CREATIVE
DO IT YOURSELF

Storage and Shelving

WARD LOCK

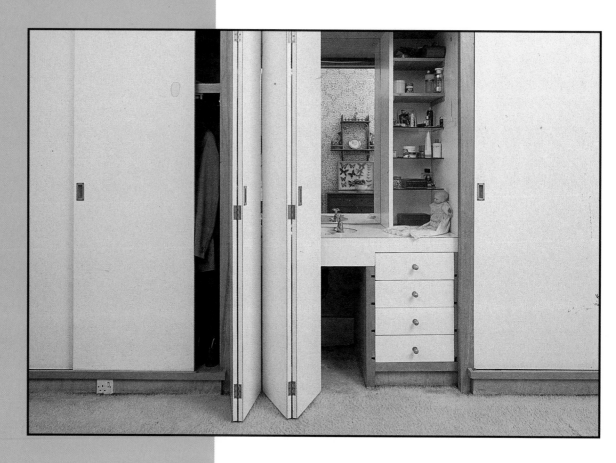

© Ward Lock Limited, 1994
A Cassell Imprint
Villiers House, 41-47 Strand, London WC2N 5JE

Based on *Successful DIY*
© Eaglemoss Publications Limited, 1994

ISBN 0 7063 7277 8

Printed in Spain by Cayfosa Industria Grafica

10 9 8 7 6 5 4 3 2 1

CONTENTS

5 **Introduction**

7 **Space-saving storage: shelves**

11 **Putting up bracket shelves**

15 **Bracketless shelving systems**

19 **Putting up alcove shelves**

25 **Putting up track shelves**

29 **Fitting glass shelving**

33 **Space-saving storage: cupboards**

37 **Built-in cupboards**

43 **Making kit drawers**

47 **Fitting out a wardrobe**

53 **Fitting sliding wardrobe doors**

59 **Modular bedroom furniture**

65 **Fitted kitchens – buying the units**

69 **Fitted kitchens – planning the layout**

73 **Fitted kitchens – fitting out the cupboards**

79 **Index**

INTRODUCTION

NOWHERE to put anything? It's a cry echoed by families everywhere. Modern builders seem to try to cram ever-smaller rooms into ever-smaller houses, while we persistently amass ever-increasing possessions that must be either stored out of sight or displayed for the world to see. The secret as far as storage is concerned is to marry efficiency with ease of access. This means creating a tailor-made home for everything: books, compact discs and videos in the living room; food, crockery, glassware and of course food in the kitchen; clothes (and perhaps toys) in the bedroom. Space must also be found for bedlinen, cleaning materials, luggage ... the list is almost endless.

Most storage needs can be met by either open shelving or closed cupboards. Shelves – whether free-standing or built into room features such as alcoves – offer ease of access, but provide no protection from dust (and grease in kitchens or steam in bathrooms); glass doors can offer a perfect compromise. Solid doors, on the other hand, can be very attractive – and mean that you don't have to keep cupboards neat and tidy. But whether you opt for open shelves or closed cupboards, aim to make the best possible use of the space available, including areas which are often regarded as dead space – walls in halls and on landings, the space beneath the stairs and so on.

The first section of this book deals with the various options open to you when putting up shelving. It explains the choices you have for each room in the house, suggesting ingenious ways of coping with particular storage and display requirements. It then covers each option in detail, with information on buying and installing shelves on individual brackets, shelves with almost no visible means of support, shelves in alcoves, shelves on adjustable tracks, and glass shelves for display purposes.

The rest of the book focuses on cupboards of every type. Again there is a look at the choices room by room, followed by information on selecting and installing built-in cupboards, adding drawers, fitting out wardrobes and installing space-saving sliding doors.

The last part of the book takes a detailed look at fitted kitchens, covering everything from the vital first stage of choosing units and planning the layout to installing and fitting out the wall and floor units and adding the vital finishing touches. Throughout the book, the emphasis is on choosing the right type of storage or display system for your needs, and installing it securely and professionally.

SPACE-SAVING STORAGE: SHELVES

Whatever the size of your home and family, stowing clutter carefully will increase the overall sense of space and avoid the frustration of not being able to find things when you want them. Take stock of what you have to store, then look around each room for ways of improving the storage already there.

Bringing order to the chaos means planning things so that the storage you choose for each room will keep pace with changing needs and contribute to an overall feeling of spaciousness. The key lies in striking a balance between display areas, where everything's there to be seen and used, and enclosed storage for the remainder which you want to keep out of sight.

Shelving falls into the first category, so start by considering the various options.

Free-standing units range in style from basic 'industrial' shelves to sophisticated 'designer' types. Simple structures with metal uprights braced by diagonal struts, and fixed or adjustable shelves, can stand free or be secured to the wall.

More stylish systems, either knock-down or ready made, are primarily for living rooms; they are often modular, allowing you to add extra units when needed, and they can generally carry heavy loads.

Track systems have the advantage of being adjustable and give you a wide choice of shelf materials.

Metal uprights come in a range of bright colours, many with coloured infill strips to give a slightly less utilitarian look.

A more attractive alternative for a living room is a wooden track system, with brackets fixed in place by screws, dowels or metal plates which are fitted into pre-drilled holes in the uprights. This type may be less easy to adjust.

Enclosed shelves which span two walls – for example, in an alcove – are a popular built-in option offering plenty of design possibilities. Stronger shelves usually have to be custom-built on batten or aluminium angle supports, but lighter shelving can make use of proprietary plastic plug or wire clip supports fitted into pre-drilled upright panels.

Unenclosed shelves can be mounted on L-shaped brackets, either individually or in groups. Bracket styles range from industrial steel and coloured enamel to scrolled wrought iron and decoratively shaped wood. Single shelf kits are also available.

Floating shelves embrace a number of patented systems in which the shelves have no visible means of support. These are useful for single shelves where space is tight, and for clean runs of display shelving.

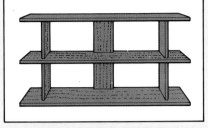

Free-standing shelves with wooden uprights for a living room.

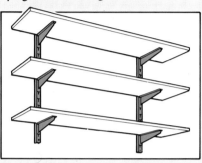

Track systems allow shelf positions to be altered.

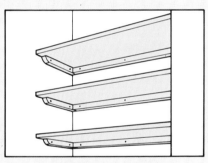

Enclosed shelves in an alcove normally sit on wooden battens.

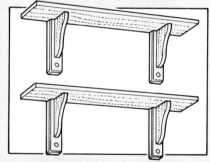

Unenclosed shelves may use metal or wooden brackets.

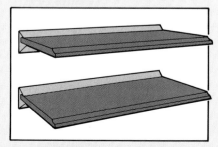

Floating shelves require one of the patented support systems.

ASSESSING YOUR NEEDS

Ask yourself these questions before making a firm decision on your shelf storage needs:

■ What do you *want* to store on shelves, and what do you *need* to store on them? Are some things better tucked away elsewhere?

■ Will the system you plan today cope with tomorrow's needs – for example – a growing collection?

■ How important is appearance? It may not be a concern in a garage or shed, but you may have to shop around for shelves with the right 'look' for living areas.

■ Do you prefer the mobility of free-standing furniture, or would built-ins suit the house better (and maybe add to its value)?

■ Will stored items vary from time to time? If so, you need the flexibility of a system with adjustable shelf heights.

■ Is variety of depth a consideration too – for example, narrow shelves for spices, but deeper ones for casseroles?

■ Do the shelves need to be easy to clean, as in a kitchen or bathroom?

■ How much can you afford in one go? On a limited budget, you might choose a system that can be added to from time to time, as funds allow.

ROOM BY ROOM PLANNING

Cast a critical eye over the items you need to store before deciding on the type of shelving and the size you need.

In a kichen, for example, the distance between shelves will be determined by the height of cookery books, storage canisters, display china and so on. In a bathroom or bedroom, you may only need a few narrow glass shelves to store toiletries and cosmetics. Children need a wider range of shelves, preferably adjustable to suit their needs as they grow.

The living room is the area which demands the most flexibility, with spaces between shelves varying from 250mm (10″) for paperbacks, to as much as 350mm (14″) for LPs, large books and folders.

Where a shelf acts as a surface for TV or hi-fi equipment, or doubles as a desk, it should be at least 500mm (20″) deep. Plan the height of the shelf above it accordingly; for example, a record deck with a hinged lid needs more space than a front-loading video recorder or CD player.

IN THE LIVING ROOM . .

In living rooms, it is important to consider shelving units as an integral part of the design plan, using finishes, colours and styles that complement the decor and period style of the room. Where there is a chimney breast, the alcoves either side make ideal recesses for shelving.

■ For a more convincingly built-in look, edge the shelves with painted wood mouldings or top them with a fascia panel to form an arch.

■ Vary the height and depth of the shelves for more visual appeal, as well as to suit the items you have to store.

■ Look out for pockets of unused space for single or floating shelves – behind a door or under windows, for example.

■ Fit narrow shelving behind a sofa, to store books or display pictures and ornaments.

■ A shelf above a radiator takes up little or no space, and helps to protect the wall from the dust marks caused by warm air rising from the radiator.

Give alcove shelves a smart finish by building in an arch.

Built-in shelves painted to blend with the rest of the decor, are one way to make the best use of available space.

A simple shelf over a radiator makes a useful telephone table.

IN THE BATHROOM . . .

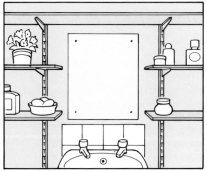

Track shelving around a mirror (above) provides useful storage.

A built-in shelf (left) makes use of space which might be wasted.

Medicines should always be kept in locked cupboards, and you'll probably want to keep cleaning materials and toilet rolls out of sight too. But other items usually benefit from being left on display, so long as the room is not too prone to condensation.

■ You may be able to fit a corner unit over the bath, or a complete run of shelves up one or both ends.

■ A narrow shelf running along the length of the bath is useful for soaps and shampoos, and hooks fitted beneath the shelf can be used to hang damp flannels.

■ Disguise ugly frosted glass with the time-honoured trick of glass shelves fitted across the window.

IN THE KITCHEN . . .

There is a definite trend towards using more open shelving in the kitchen – if only to display china or break up clinical rows of fitted cupboards. But beware you don't actually *reduce* the amount of storage space – you cannot usually stack away as much on shelves as you can in cupboards.

■ Fit open shelves in awkward spaces between units – for china and storage jars at a high level, or for casseroles and pans below the level of the work surface.

■ Shelves which are to be used to display plates should have a lip or groove to prevent them slipping forwards.

■ There's often space for a shelf over a window to store rarely used items.

■ In a kitchen with a dining area, don't forget the walls around this in your hunt for extra shelf space.

■ If you plan to store dry goods like flour, rice, tea and spices on open shelves, collect matching storage jars so they look attractive and tidy.

■ Space below wall cupboards is ideal for spice-jar shelves.

High level shelving *provides acessible storage.*

IN THE BEDROOM . . .

The bed is almost invariably the most dominant item in a bedroom, so plan your storage around it.

■ A shelf above the head of a double bed can replace space-consuming bedside tables.

■ Where a single bed is placed against a wall, consider fixing a set of narrow shelves above it for books and ornaments. A wider shelf at the very top can be used for items like sports bags or rarely used hobby equipment.

■ In shared bedrooms, place the beds end to end (or in an L-shaped configuration) with a tall, free-standing shelving unit between them.

■ In very small bedrooms, a complete wall of open storage to either side of and above the door makes use of space which would probably otherwise go to waste, with minimal loss of floor space.

■ In children's rooms, consider their needs as they grow. For example, a wide adjustable shelf could serve as a changing table for a baby, a painting table for a toddler, or a desk for a teenager.

Free-standing shelves *(above) make a serviceable room divider.*
Are you making the most *of the space around the bedhead? A shelf (left) can replace cumbersome bedside tables.*

TAKE ANOTHER LOOK

If you've checked out the main rooms in the house and find they still can't meet all your shelf storage needs, take another look – there are bound to be places you've overlooked, or wouldn't normally consider as sites for shelves.

■ Start by looking up: many rooms have space for shelves around the top – across the top of the window, or high above the bath for example.

■ Have you made good use of the space under the stairs? A series of shelves against the wall makes a useful store for cleaning materials,

and you can always screen them with a blind if you don't want items to be on display. Boxes and baskets are also useful devices for storing unsightly items on shelves.

■ In many homes there is space at the top of the stairs which goes to waste. It may be possible to fit shelves on the return wall above the stairwell, or a slim bookshelf (for paperbacks) on the landing, without loosing a significant amount of floor space.

■ Don't forget to make use of the space *under* shelves – for example,

by fitting cup hooks or hanging wire baskets on runners.

■ If a large room is used for different activities – for example a living room diner or bed-sitting room, consider using open, floor to ceiling shelving to demarcate the two areas.

■ Don't forget that garages and outbuildings equipped with low-cost floor to ceiling shelving can often take much of the spill-over from the house – tools, decorating materials, and rarely used kitchen utensils which you want to store.

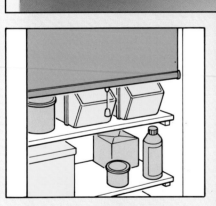

Under the shelf: under-shelf baskets help to make extra use of the space between shelves. Use them inside cupboards (left), or on open shelving if appropriate.

Look up: you can usually fit shelves at a high level (below) for books, magazines and sewing baskets, for example. Intersperse objects with plants and ornaments for a more decorative effect.

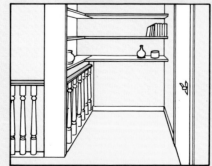

Shelved and screened: blinds, boxes and baskets can all be used to hide away items like cleaning materials, paint tins and tools.

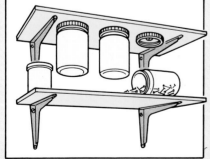

Screw-top trick: empty coffee jars make useful containers for screws and nails. Glue or screw the tops to the underside of the shelf, then simply unscrew the jars to get at the contents.

On the landing: look at the space carefully – it is often possible to fit shelves for a work area, or there may be sufficient room to store books at the top of the stairs.

Dividing lines: use floor to ceiling shelves to divide the kitchen area from the dining area in a dual-purpose room. Rails prevent china and glass from being knocked off.

PUTTING UP
BRACKET SHELVES

If you only want a few fixed shelves, separate brackets are an ideal choice. They are often cheaper and easier to fit than track systems – although this advantage is reduced every time you add another shelf. And because there is a much wider range of styles, both brackets and shelves can be chosen to suit your decorations.

Bracket styles range from cheap and functional to stylish or ornate. The basic options are detailed below, and overleaf is a guide to what to use where. You can buy your shelving boards separately, but some brackets are sold in complete 'shelf packs' with boards to match.

Alternatives Separate brackets aren't a sensible choice if you want a run of stacked shelving because of the difficulty of lining up all the holes – consider a track system instead. Conventional brackets may also be hard to fit directly above objects such as radiators.

Shelves on brackets provide quick, convenient storage – and can look as stylish as you want.

.... Shopping List ....

Brackets come in several patterns. The size and number needed depend on the size of the shelves and the weight they will support (see overleaf):

Utility pressed steel brackets are a good choice for workrooms or garages and can be painted.

'Streamlined' steel or plastic-covered brackets are strong and inexpensive. The finish is good enough for display shelves.

'Wrought iron' brackets made of steel or aluminium in various finishes are reasonably strong but can be tricky to fit.

Cast-iron and brass brackets can be stylish, but are expensive.

Wooden brackets are sometimes sold separately but are more often part of complete 'shelf packs'.

Shelves Natural wood, man-made boards and glass can all be used. See overleaf for details of what to consider when choosing.

Fixings Normally you need two or three screws and wallplugs per bracket to fix to the wall, and two or three to fix the shelf. Use the heaviest screws that fit the bracket. They should project about 38mm (1½″) into the wall and up to three quarters of the way through the shelf.

Tools: Drill with masonry and wood bits, screwdriver, tape measure, spirit level (and possibly a plumbline), plus a saw and try square if you are going to cut and trim shelves.

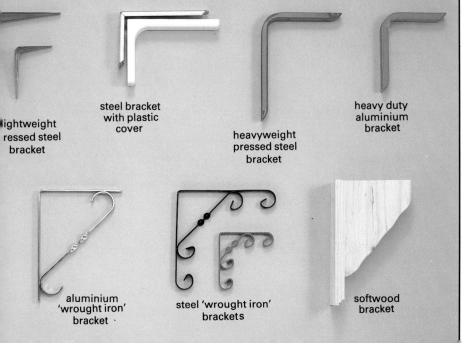

lightweight pressed steel bracket

steel bracket with plastic cover

heavyweight pressed steel bracket

heavy duty aluminium bracket

aluminium 'wrought iron' bracket

steel 'wrought iron' brackets

softwood bracket

CHOOSING SHELVES AND BRACKETS

Whatever type of brackets you want, consider these points:

Strength For maximum load bearing, all brackets depend on secure fixings to a sound wall. If they have an instruction sheet, this may say how much weight they can take. If there are no details, play safe by fitting them at the 'heavy load' spacings given in the following sections.

Size Most brackets have one long and one short arm – the long arm normally goes on the wall. (Plastic covered brackets have the short arm on the wall, and 'wrought iron' are usually equal lengths.) If there is a choice of sizes, pick brackets which support all but about 25mm (1″) of the shelf. Too much overhang can overload them.

Number How many brackets you need per shelf depends both on the type of wall, and on type and length of the shelves.

On solid walls, brackets can go anywhere; space them to suit the shelves so that there's no risk of bowing (see following sections).

On hollow walls (plasterboard on a timber frame), the brackets must be screwed direct to the timber studs – usually spaced at 400mm (16″) centres. Don't screw to the plasterboard itself.

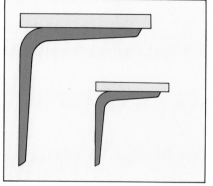

Where there is a choice of bracket sizes, choose ones which support nearly the whole depth of the shelf. Otherwise you risk overloading them.

Use recommended bracket spacing. Where possible, set the brackets in from the ends of the shelf so that the weight over the ends balances the weight in the middle.

WOODEN SHELVING

Wooden brackets look good when teamed with natural timber shelving – they are often sold with matching boards as a complete 'shelf pack'. However, for heavy loads, it may be wiser to opt for metal brackets, which tend to be stronger than wood.

If you buy the shelves separately, choose from 19 or 25mm (¾ or 1″) thick solid softwood (hardwood is hard to find and very expensive), or use laminated softwood boards. The latter are often a better buy since they tend to be free of blemishes and come in various shelf widths. All types need to be varnished or painted.

BRACKET SPACINGS
(for a solid wall only):

Board thickness	Medium load	Heavy load
19mm (¾″)	700mm (27″)	500mm (20″)
25mm (1″)	900mm (36″)	700mm (27″)
28mm (1⅛″)*	900mm (36″)	700mm (27″)

* only available in laminated softwood

Wooden brackets and shelves can be used to create a country kitchen look.

MAN-MADE BOARDS

You can cut shelf boards yourself from a single sheet, but it's usually easier to buy shelf-width boards ready finished with a veneer or melamine coating. You can also get 'shelf packs' with matching coloured shelves and brackets.

If cutting your own, choose from wood veneered or coated chipboard, or MDF (minimum thickness 16mm – ⅝″). Alternatively, use plywood or blockboard (minimum thickness 12mm – ½″ if good quality, otherwise 16mm – ⅝″).

Finish the edges of home-made chipboard and blockboard shelves with iron-on strip or hardwood lipping. Fill the edges of plywood shelves (unless varnishing) with fine surface filler and rub down. All wood-faced boards need painting or varnishing.

BRACKET SPACINGS
(for a solid wall only):

Board thickness	Medium load	Heavy load
12mm (½″)*	400mm (16″)	not advisable
16mm (⅝″)	600mm (24″)	400mm (16″)
19mm (¾″)	700mm (27″)	500mm (20″)
25mm (1″)	900mm (36″)	700mm (27″)

* plywood/blockboard only

Trade tip

Uneven walls

6 Most metal brackets have arms which are long enough to span minor bumps without causing serious misalignment. But if the wall is very uneven, it may be hard to fix where you need to.

Instead, use short lengths of 50×25mm (2×1″) batten as fixing plates. Screw them to the wall where you like, but don't let the screws obstruct the bracket fixings. 9

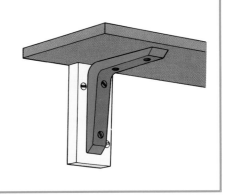

Melamine faced chipboard and plastic covered brackets make for bright, easy-care shelving.

GLASS SHELVES

Make sure the glass is up to the job and out of childrens' reach. It must be at least 6mm (¼″) thick for light display shelves, and 9mm (⅜″) thick for heavier loads. Have the edges ground and polished by the supplier.

'Wrought iron' brackets are a good choice for glass shelves, but may be tricky to fit as the screws are hard to get at – a stubby screwdriver helps. Use heavy duty ones for thicker glass and stick the shelves in place with *glass fixing pads*. These have a self adhesive backing and are designed to cushion the glass.

Brackets for glass bathroom shelves usually fit over the ends of the shelf, which may be included as part of a kit.

BRACKET SPACINGS
(for a solid wall only):

Glass thickness	Medium load	Heavy load
6mm (¼″)	400mm (16″)	not advisable
9mm (⅜″)	700mm (27″)	500mm (20″)

Glass shelving is light and unobtrusive.

PUTTING UP THE SHELVES

Lightweight shelves are best fitted with their brackets before fixing to the wall.

■ Mark the bracket positions on the underside of the shelf, drill pilot holes, and screw the brackets in place.

■ Offer up the complete assembly to the wall with a spirit level on top. Check the alignment, then mark the bracket fixing holes. Drill and plug.

Heavy shelves are easier to fit if you fix the brackets to the wall first.

■ Mark the bracket positions underneath the shelf. Check where one end bracket falls on the wall and position it to mark the fixing holes.

■ Drill and plug the wall and fix the bracket in place.

■ Support the shelf (or a straight length of batten) on the fixed bracket with a spirit level on top. Check for level, then mark the position of the other end bracket.

■ Remove the shelf and fix the second bracket to the wall.

■ Rest the shelf on both brackets and mark the positions of the other brackets. Fix them to the wall, then screw the shelf to all the brackets.

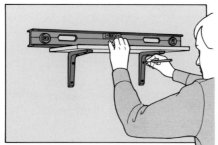

A small shelf is easier to fit if you screw the brackets to it first. Position the shelf with the aid of a spirit level, then mark the bracket fixings.

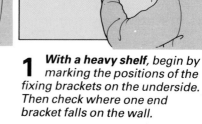

1 **With a heavy shelf**, begin by marking the positions of the fixing brackets on the underside. Then check where one end bracket falls on the wall.

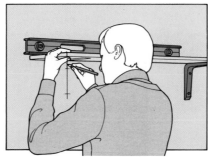

2 Fix this end bracket in place. Offer up the shelf (or a straight batten) with a spirit level on top and mark the other end bracket's position.

3 Add intervening brackets with the shelf resting in place. Check that each bracket supports the shelf correctly, then mark its fixing position on the wall.

■ PROBLEM SOLVER■

Aligning several shelves

If you need to stack shelves one above the other, but don't want a track system, there are two methods of fixing brackets:

Fixing to battens first makes it easier to align the brackets and avoids having to drill a lot of holes in the wall.

Mark the bracket positions with the battens laid together to ensure they line up. Screw the brackets in place, then screw each batten to the wall at 300mm (12″) intervals.

The backs of the shelves must be notched to fit over the battens if you want the shelves to sit flush with the wall.

Fixing independently is neater, and means the shelves don't need to be notched. However, it is more difficult to get the shelves in line, which is essential if the result is to look good.

Mark out the first shelf and use it as a template to mark all the others. Fix the first pair of brackets to the wall and hang a plumbline from each. Then use the lines as a guide to fixing the rows of brackets below.

To align separate shelves (below), fix the top set of brackets and then use plumblines to gauge the positions of the brackets in the rows below.

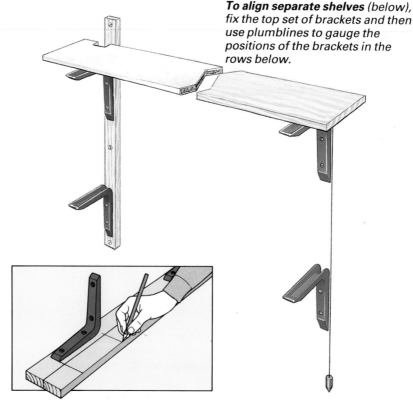

A stack of shelves is easier to align if you fit the brackets to lengths of batten first.

Notch the backs of the shelves to fit over the battens. Fit the brackets to both battens together to guarantee even spacing.

BRACKETLESS SHELVING SYSTEMS

There are plenty of different ways to support shelves using brackets, tracks or home-made batten arrangements. But many of these systems are none too easy on the eye, particularly if you only want a single shelf. And there are other situations – above a radiator for example – where there simply isn't room to fit conventional supports.

'Bracketless' shelving systems are designed to solve both problems by providing (or appearing to provide) steady support along the back edge of the shelf alone. This makes them perfect for single shelves and awkward corners where space is tight. It also means that your eye is naturally drawn to what's on the shelf, rather than to what holds it up.

Patent 'bracketless' systems come and go, but the three described below are tried and tested, and reasonably widely available. Choose whichever suits your purpose – and shelf material – the best.

Aluminium channel systems are one way to fix a shelf securely – yet almost invisibly.

.... Shopping List ....

Support system There are three basic options:

Aluminium channel is a continuous metal extrusion which is screwed to the wall behind the shelf. The rear edge of the shelf is pressed home into a special retaining groove which grips and supports it firmly. Various sizes are available to suit a range of thicknesses.

Cantilever brackets are impact-resistant plastic shelf supports for use on masonry walls. Each bracket has a hardened steel pin which is sunk into a pre-drilled hole, leaving a small fixing flange which is hidden when the shelves are fitted. Most types of shelving board are suitable.

Concealed hanging plates are two-part metal fittings which attach to the back edges of shelves with integral bookends (the plates work on a cantilever principle, so they must go on the bookends – fixing to the edge of the shelf won't work).

Shelf materials Most standard shelving boards are suitable, although aluminium channel restricts your choice of thickness – see overleaf. Laminated softwood and edged melamine faced boards are good choices requiring minimal finishing.

Concealed hanging plates can be used on home-made bookend shelves, but they are also sold as a complete kit.

Wall fixings Wallplugs and countersunk screws (often supplied with the supports) are needed for masonry walls. Use countersunk woodscrews for fixing to the studs of timber-framed walls.

Tools checklist: Drill and bits (masonry drill size may be critical, so check the instructions carefully), tape measure, spirit level, screwdriver, panel saw for cutting shelves. You may also need a junior hacksaw, soft-faced hammer/mallet, bradawl, plane and scribing tools.

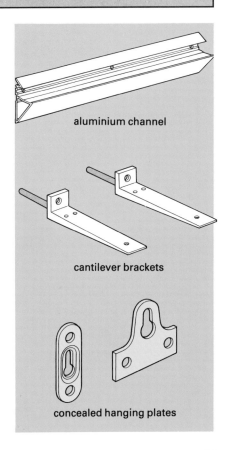

aluminium channel

cantilever brackets

concealed hanging plates

USING ALUMINIUM CHANNEL

Aluminium channel is smart and unobtrusive, simple to level and fix, and easy to keep clean. The system is available in a number of colours and comes in a range of standard lengths which can be sawn to size if required. Plastic push-in caps conceal the cut ends if visible.

Standard channels accept shelf boards 15mm (⅝″) thick, while some suppliers offer a contract range designed to fit 19mm (¾″) boards. There is also a special profile for 6mm (¼″) glass shelves. Packs include end caps, screws and plugs.

Planning points

■ Because the shelf is supported along its entire length, it can carry surprisingly heavy loads. For example, a 15mm shelf 1220mm (4′) long and 300mm (12″) wide can carry an evenly distributed load of 60kg (132lbs) if fixed to brickwork, or 20kg (44lbs) on timber-framed walls.
■ Shelf thickness is restricted to the available channel sizes.
■ The channels work out comparatively expensive on long runs of shelving.
■ Channels are easily cut to size, and can be drilled for extra screw holes when fixing to the studs on a timber-framed wall. Do not rely on cavity fixings.

What you need

■ Channel of required length plus fixings and end caps.
■ Shelving of the appropriate material and thickness, plus (for chipboard) edging strip. Finishing materials may also be needed.
■ Glass shelves must be cut to order from a glazier. Specify 6mm float glass and ask for the edges to be rounded and polished.

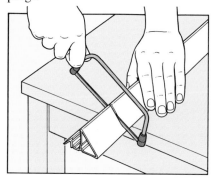

1 Cut the channel to length if need be using a junior hacksaw. On a timber-framed wall, find the studs and drill corresponding holes in the channel.

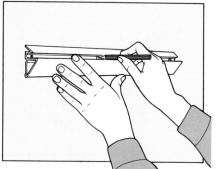

2 Offer up the channel to the wall and mark the central fixing hole. Drill (and on a masonry wall, plug), then drive the fixing screw part-way in.

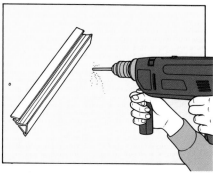

3 Swing the channel horizontal, check the level and mark the other holes. Swing it aside to drill the holes, then back into position to fix the screws.

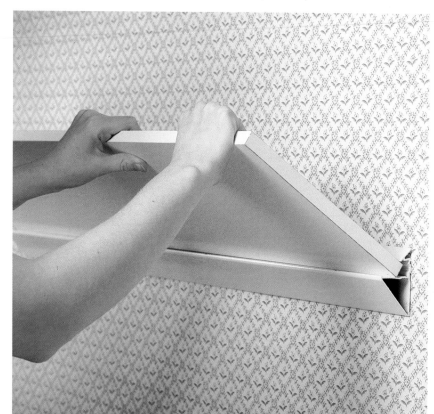

4 Insert the rear edge of the shelf into the channel, then rock it down to the horizontal and tap it fully home, protecting the edge of the shelf with scrap wood if necessary. Fit the caps to cover the ends.

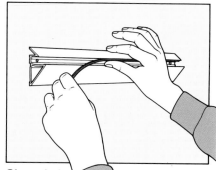

Glass shelves need a special version of the channel. Slide the sealing strip supplied into the top of the channel before positioning the shelf.

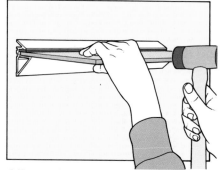

Offer up the glass shelf and insert in the channel. Then carefully tap the shelf fully home using a rubber mallet or a wooden mallet and a soft pad.

USING CANTILEVER BRACKETS

This system is a clever variation on using conventional L-shaped brackets; the only limitation is that the cantilever support pins are not intended for timber-framed walls. Otherwise, plan your shelf sizes and bracket positions as for any other type of bracket (see pages 11-14 for details).

The brackets are sold in packs of two, complete with fixings, and come in two sizes – 115mm (4½") and 190mm (7"). The projecting support pin is 50mm (2") long in both cases, but is 6.5mm in diameter on the smaller bracket and 8mm on the larger one.

Planning points

■ You can use the brackets with shelves of any material and thickness; the 115mm bracket is for shelves up to 150mm (6") wide, the 190mm bracket takes shelves up to 230mm (9") wide.
■ Fixing requires some care, since the hole for the cantilever pin must be drilled precisely at right angles to the wall surface.
■ If you want the back edge of the shelf to fit flush, it must be notched to accept the retaining flanges on the brackets.

What you need

■ Brackets of the appropriate length.
■ Screws for securing the shelf to the brackets.
■ A suitable masonry drill – No. 12 for the small bracket, No. 16 for the larger one.

Cantilever brackets project a mere 16mm (⅝") below the shelf and are scarcely noticeable.

1 Mark the bracket positions and drill 60mm (2½") deep holes of the required diameter in the wall. Make sure that they are at right angles to the surface.

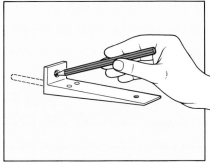

2 Push the pin into the hole with a twisting action until the flange meets the wall. Mark the screw position, remove the bracket, then drill and plug.

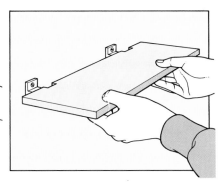

3 Screw the brackets in place and offer up the shelf, notching and scribing its rear edge if necessary. Drill fixing holes and screw to the brackets.

USING HANGING PLATES

Two-part hanging plates are primarily designed for shelf units. One part is screwed to the rear edge of the shelf unit, the other to the wall, and the two interlock so that the unit can be hooked in place.

Keyhole glass plates can be used in a similar way. Each plate is screwed to the rear edge of the unit, allowing the keyhole to be hooked over the head of a countersunk screw driven into the wall surface to provide a virtually invisible means of support.

Planning points

■ Plates are inexpensive and easy to use for any shelf unit which has end frames. They cannot be used for a single shelf unless this has integral bookends.
■ The loadbearing performance depends mainly on the strength of the fixings made into the rear edge of the shelf unit itself.
■ Accurate positioning is needed to ensure a level mounting – it helps if there are two of you.
■ Since the spacing of the uprights dictates the position of the plates, mounting the unit on timber-framed walls can be awkward unless the unit's width matches the spacing of the studs.

What you need

■ Suitable shelf unit or shelf with integral bookends.
■ A pair of interlocking hanging plates or keyhole glass plates.
■ Fixing screws and wallplugs.

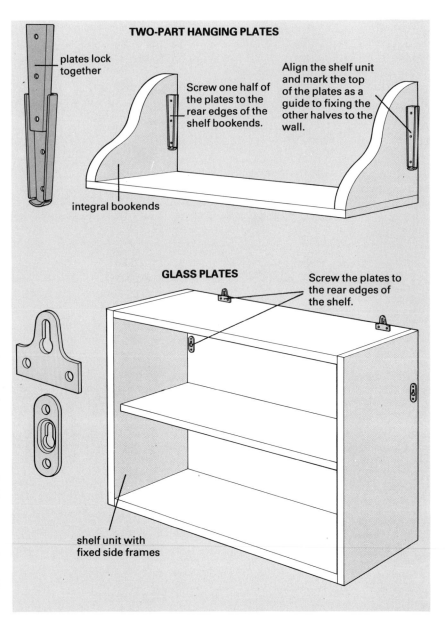

TWO-PART HANGING PLATES

plates lock together

Screw one half of the plates to the rear edges of the shelf bookends.

Align the shelf unit and mark the top of the plates as a guide to fixing the other halves to the wall.

integral bookends

GLASS PLATES

Screw the plates to the rear edges of the shelf.

shelf unit with fixed side frames

PROBLEM SOLVER

Radiator shelves

Although theoretically you can use any of the methods previously described to fit a shelf above a radiator, drilling fixing holes may prove awkward. A much simpler solution is to use specially designed *radiator shelf brackets* which slot down behind the radiator itself and simply wedge in place against the wall.

First of all, make sure that the radiator itself is firmly fixed, and that it sits parallel to the wall. You should also select your shelf material with care: the rising heat is likely to warp natural timber, so man-made boards such as faced chipboard, plywood or blockboard are a much better choice in this situation.

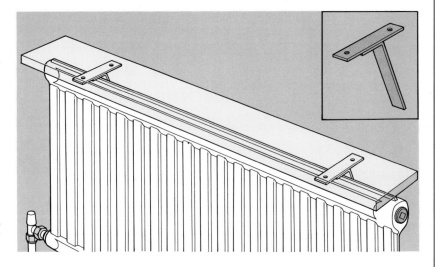

Radiator shelf brackets simply screw to the underside of the shelf board, though make sure they don't coincide with the fixing bracket positions. The brackets wedge against the wall when the shelf is pushed into place.

PUTTING UP ALCOVE SHELVES

Putting up shelves in alcoves is a time-honoured way of using space that might otherwise go to waste – and this form of storage is perfectly suited to books, records, ornaments and hi-fi equipment.

Over the years, people have devised countless ways of arranging and supporting alcove shelving, but most are variations on one of the five options described overleaf.

....Shopping List....

Shelf materials: Work out the size and number of shelves as shown below. Then see overleaf for the options on boards and finishes.
Supports Work out how many shelves to put up, as shown below. Then check the chart overleaf to size up the supports and other fixings.
Wall fixings: Wallplugs, No.8 screws (to gauge length, add 32mm (1¼") to thickness of what you're fixing).
Tools: Panel saw, drill and bits, tenon saw, tape measure, spirit level, screwdriver. You may also need a junior hacksaw, wood chisel, Surform plane or scribing tools.

Alcove shelves provide an ideal way to store large quantities of books.

DESIGNING ALCOVE SHELVES

Start by measuring the alcove. If you want to put up more than one shelf, draw a sketch plan showing the alcove dimensions.

Although you can put the shelves at any heights you like, there are some practical guidelines:
■ If you are putting shelves in a pair of alcoves, keep the shelf spacings the same on both sides.
■ Wider-spaced shelves tend to look best at or below worktop/table height – around 750–900mm (30–36"). Set the first level of shelves here, then work out the spacings up and down.
■ Small paperbacks need 200mm (8") height and 125mm (5") depth.
■ Large illustrated books need a spacing of around 330mm (13") and a depth of 225–250mm (9–10").
■ You may want one shelf spaced at around 330mm (13") below the next, to hold hi-fi speakers, records, or a small TV. This shelf needs to be 300mm (12") or more in depth.

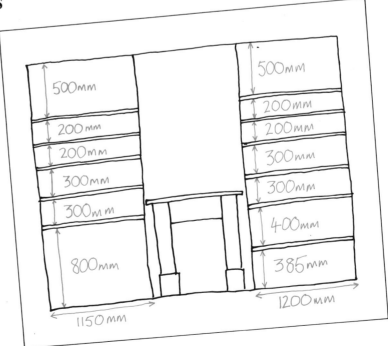

A sketch plan helps you keep track of what you need to buy, and acts as a reminder of the shelf spacings when you come to mark them out.

CHOOSING SHELVES AND SUPPORTS

There's a wide range of options for both the shelf boards themselves and the way you support them.

Choosing shelf boards

The panel below shows what materials can be used, depending on the look you want. Your choice will also be affected by:

What you want to store. Books and records are heavy, so need boards which resist warping. If the books are large OR the span is over 900mm (3'), follow the appropriate Bracing Guide and only use boards rated as suitable for 'heavy duty'.

On the other hand, shelves for lightweight ornaments should be as thin as possible so that they don't detract from what's on them.

The size of the shelves. Some materials only come in small sizes, while boards which come in large sheets are wasteful if you are only fitting a few shelves.

Choosing supports

The chart opposite shows the support options available. Again, your choice may depend on:

What you want to store. Small shelves for ornaments need light, unobtrusive supports, but for anything heavier choose one of the stronger systems (options 1, 2 and 3). If you are storing a lot of large books or other heavy items, OR the span is over 900mm (3'), use a back batten/aluminium angle or extra brackets. If you think your storage needs may change, an adjustable system could make sense.

The depth of the alcove. If you are fitting deep shelves in a very shallow alcove, end supports (ie options 1, 2, 3 and 5) may not offer sufficient bracing. Unless at least two thirds of the depth is supported, option 4 is more reliable.

The condition of the walls. Some systems (eg options 3, 5) are well suited to walls which are uneven and out of square with each other.

How the walls are made. Chimney breast walls are always solid, but if the other walls are hollow, options 1 and 2 (which allow you to fix to the studs at any point) are better; don't rely on cavity wall fixings.

The look of the shelves. Aim to choose a system that's in keeping with the style of the room. Track shelves, for example, can look out of place in a traditional setting, while batten supports may not suit a more modern, streamlined look.

CHOOSING SHELF BOARDS

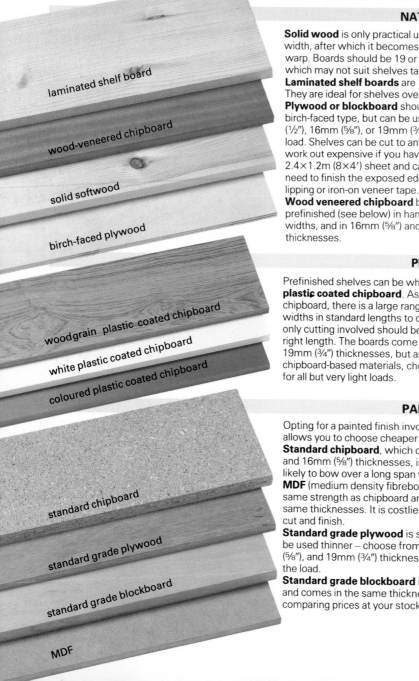

laminated shelf board

wood-veneered chipboard

solid softwood

birch-faced plywood

woodgrain plastic coated chipboard

white plastic coated chipboard

coloured plastic coated chipboard

standard chipboard

standard grade plywood

standard grade blockboard

MDF

NATURAL FINISH

Solid wood is only practical up to a 225mm (9") width, after which it becomes costly and liable to warp. Boards should be 19 or 25mm (¾ or 1") thick, which may not suit shelves taking ornaments.
Laminated shelf boards are 19mm (¾") thick. They are ideal for shelves over 225mm (9") wide.
Plywood or blockboard should be the high quality birch-faced type, but can be used thinner – 12mm (½"), 16mm (⅝"), or 19mm (¾"), depending on the load. Shelves can be cut to any width, but may work out expensive if you have to buy a full-size 2.4×1.2m (8×4') sheet and can't use it all. You also need to finish the exposed edges with solid wood lipping or iron-on veneer tape.
Wood veneered chipboard boards come prefinished (see below) in handy lengths and widths, and in 16mm (⅝") and 19mm (¾") thicknesses.

BRACING GUIDE
Solid softwood (19mm): add extra bracing over 600mm (24") for medium duty, or 450mm (18") for heavy duty.
Solid softwood (25mm): add extra bracing over 750mm (30") for heavy duty.
Laminated board (19mm): add extra bracing over 750mm (30") for heavy duty.
Plywood and blockboard (see below for all sizes)
Veneered chipboard (see *Other boards* below)

PREFINISHED

Prefinished shelves can be white or coloured **plastic coated chipboard**. As with wood veneered chipboard, there is a large range of pre-cut 'shelf' widths in standard lengths to choose from, so the only cutting involved should be trimming to the right length. The boards come in 16mm (⅝") and 19mm (¾") thicknesses, but as with other chipboard-based materials, choose the thicker size for all but very light loads.

BRACING GUIDE
Coated chipboard (see *Other boards* below)

PAINTED FINISH

Opting for a painted finish involves more work, but allows you to choose cheaper material.
Standard chipboard, which comes in 19mm (¾") and 16mm (⅝") thicknesses, is economical but likely to bow over a long span with a heavy load.
MDF (medium density fibreboard) is about the same strength as chipboard and comes in the same thicknesses. It is costlier, but much easier to cut and finish.
Standard grade plywood is stronger and so can be used thinner – choose from 12mm (½"), 16mm (⅝"), and 19mm (¾") thicknesses, depending on the load.
Standard grade blockboard is similar to plywood and comes in the same thicknesses. It's worth comparing prices at your stockist.

BRACING GUIDE
Plywood (12mm): add extra bracing over 600mm (24") for medium duty.
Plywood (16mm): add extra bracing over 600mm (24") for medium duty, or 450mm (18") for heavy duty.
Plywood (19mm): add extra bracing over 750mm (30") for heavy duty.
Other boards (16mm): add extra bracing over 600mm (24") for medium duty.
Other boards (19mm): add extra bracing over 750mm (30") for medium duty.

SUPPORT SYSTEMS

	DESCRIPTION	PROS & CONS	WHAT YOU NEED
Option 1: Wooden battens (medium/heavy duty) 	Shelves are supported on a pair of wooden battens screwed to the walls. The ends of the battens can be angled or curved to make them less noticeable. For heavy loads or wide spans, add a third batten along the back wall.	Inexpensive and easy to fit if the walls are smooth and more or less square to each other. On hollow walls, the battens allow you to make fixings wherever you want, so there is no need to worry about the stud spacing.	Softwood batten (the thickness of the shelf material by twice the thickness of the shelf material). Wallplugs and screws to fix batten. To fix the shelves to the batten you also need 12mm (½″) No.6 screws, plus three or four 3-hole glass plates per shelf.
Option 2: Aluminium angle (medium/heavy duty) 	Shelves are supported on lengths of L-section aluminium angle, now widely available from hardware and superstores. As with battens, you can use two or three strips per shelf depending on the load and shelf span.	Less noticeable than battens, but slightly trickier to fit. Like battens, best suited to alcove walls which are even and true.	Aluminium angle the same width as the thickness of the shelving. Wallplugs and screws.
Option 3: Tracks/brackets (medium/heavy duty) 	Shelves are supported on a proprietary track system, or on purpose-made metal or wooden shelf brackets attached to batten 'tracks'. Use in pairs for light loads/narrow alcoves; add a third support on wide spans and heavy loads.	Tracks fully adjustable and easier to fit than brackets, but decorative effect of brackets may be preferable. Cost of parts must be borne in mind. Best suited to uneven walls where shelves can't be an exact fit.	Proprietary track system, or brackets (2–3 per shelf) and 50×19mm (2×¾″) softwood batten supports. Wallplugs and screws and 19mm (¾″) No.6 screws.
Option 4: Bookcase strip (light duty or narrow spans) 	Shelves are supported on side walls only using bookcase strip – a mini track system with adjustable hook supports.	Easy-to-fit supports are unobtrusive and fully adjustable, but unsuitable for uneven walls, wide shelves or heavy loads. Shelves cannot be fixed in place.	Bookcase strip system (2 per side wall)
Option 5: Plug-in shelf supports (light duty or narrow spans) 	Alcove is lined with boards scribed to fit. Shelves are supported on side walls only; holes drilled in lining accept plug-in shelf supports designed for fitting in cupboards.	Trickiest option, but worth considering if alcove walls are in very poor condition. Once lining is in place, shelf supports are easy to fit. Drilling extra holes gives full adjustability.	Suitable lining material (eg chipboard, plywood, blockboard, MDF), slips of thin batten, hardboard or cardboard for packing, 50mm (2″) No.8 screws for fixing, plug-in shelf supports.

FITTING WOODEN BATTENS

Cut batten supports to length to suit the shelves and the depth of the alcove. Side battens don't have to finish flush with the front edge – stopping them a little way back makes them less obtrusive. You can also shape the ends by sawing off at an angle or smoothing into a curve using a Surform plane.

After cutting, drill fixing holes in the side battens at 75mm (3″) inter- vals and in the back batten at 300mm (12″) intervals. Fix them in the sequence shown so that you can be sure the shelves will sit level.

Fixing the shelves to the battens is optional, but advisable unless they are heavily weighed down. Glass plates are best where you can see the fixings, but above eye level you can simply screw the shelves to their battens from above.

Trade tip
Keeping shelves flat

❝ If you're fitting a back batten, fix the side battens first, then leave the shelf in place while you mark the fixing holes on the wall. This way, you can be sure the shelf sits level on all three battens. ❞

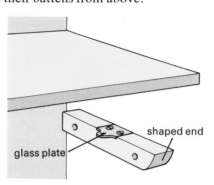

cut end

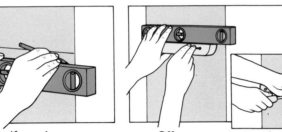

glass plate   shaped end

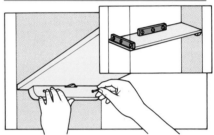

1 Mark the shelf spacings on one side of the alcove, not forgetting to allow for the thickness of the shelves themselves.

2 Offer up one pre-cut batten (allow for a back batten if fitted), level it, and mark the fixing holes. Drill and plug the wall, then screw in place.

3 Resting the shelf on the fixed batten, offer up the other side batten. Check for level both ways, then mark the fixing holes and screw to the wall.

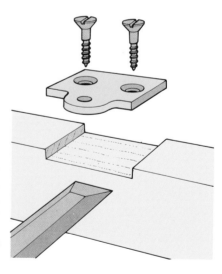

Fix shelves with glass plates where the tops are below eye level and likely to show; use 1 per side batten, 1–2 along a back batten. Chisel shallow recesses for the plates in the battens, screw in place, then refit the shelf to mark the fixing holes.

Wooden battens (left) which are painted the same colour as the shelves are neat and unobtrusive.

USING ALUMINIUM ANGLE

Aluminium angle is easily cut to fit using a junior hacksaw. Smooth the ends with a file or coarse wet and dry abrasive paper.

Drill the screw fixing holes in the side pieces at 75mm (3″) intervals and in the back piece at 300mm (12″) intervals, supporting the angle on an offcut of wood. To stop the drill bit wandering, pop-mark the holes with a centre punch or nail.

Don't forget to allow 4mm (⅛″) for the thickness of the angle when cutting the shelves to fit (see overleaf). Otherwise, follow the same fitting sequence as for wooden battens. Fix the shelves to the angle by screwing through from below with 12mm (½″) No.4 chipboard screws.

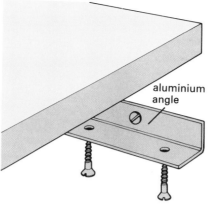

aluminium angle

Aluminium angle is a strong and much less conspicuous alternative to batten supports. Saw it to length and pre-drill the fixing holes.

USING BOOKCASE STRIP

Two strips per side should be sufficient for all but the largest alcoves, but they look best if they run the full height. Space the strips a quarter of the way in from the front and back of the shelf.

Screw the strips to the wall as you would shelf tracks, using a spirit level to check for plumb. The supports can be hooked into the strips at any height.

Cut the shelves 8mm (⅜″) narrower than the alcove to allow clearance for the strips; this is easier than trying to notch the shelves.

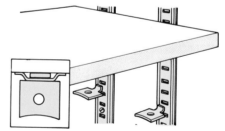

Bookcase strip comes in brass and silver finish and can be screwed directly onto even wall surfaces. Fit clip-in supports to take the ends of the shelf boards.

TRACK AND BRACKET SYSTEMS

When fitting a track or bracket system, choose brackets with a span that suits the depth of the shelves. The only special consideration is how you space the supports.

If there are two sets, aim to position them a quarter of the way in from either side of the alcove. But if this means that the supports exceed their recommended spacing, include a third set running down the middle of the alcove and position the outer two sets one-sixth of the way in from the edges.

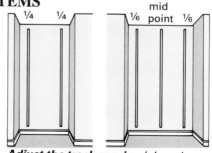

Adjust the track spacing (above) to suit the alcove width. Shelf heights can be varied (right) depending upon what you wish to display.

CUTTING SHELVES TO FIT

Don't attempt to cut all the shelves to the same size unless:
1 The walls of the alcove are even and true (or you have lined them).
2 The walls aren't true, but you are using a track system and need adjustable shelves. In this case cut the shelves so they all fit the width of the alcove at its narrowest point, allowing a small clearance.

In all other situations it's best to measure and cut each shelf individually. You can do this conventionally, using a tape or measuring sticks; but since the sides of the alcove are probably uneven, as well as out of true, it's safer to use the template method shown below.

Trade tip

Perfect fit

❛ To be sure of an exact fit, make up a template for each shelf in turn using an offcut of board and some pieces of card.

Get a helper to hold the offcut against the back of the alcove at shelf height while you place pieces of card on top and slide them against the sides to mimic the alcove's shape. Tape the card to the board, then remove it and use it to mark the shelf board for cutting. ❜

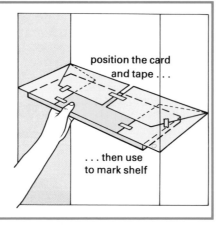

position the card and tape . . .

. . . then use to mark shelf

If the shelves don't need to fit exactly, use a pair of sticks joined with rubber bands to check the minimum width of the alcove, then allow 6mm (¼″) clearance.

◾ PROBLEM SOLVER ◾

Alcove not square

If, as is often the case in older houses, the alcove sides are seriously out of true, it's sensible to choose Option 5 – line the sides with boards, then fit plug-in shelf supports (as found inside fitted units).

Select a rigid material for the lining (you may want to match it to the shelving), so that there's no danger of the boards bowing out of shape as they are being fixed; 16mm (⅝″) plywood, and 19mm (¾″) blockboard, MDF or chipboard are possible options.

Start by cutting and scribing the boards to fit. Whether they run the full height of the alcove or finish at the skirting is up to you: if the skirting looks easy to remove, a full-height lining will be neater.

Fix the boards at roughly 450mm (18″) intervals, using 50mm (2″) No.6 screws. Space the screws at 100mm (4″) centres, or to coincide with stud positions.

Pack behind the boards to bring them vertical as you screw them to the wall – use thin battens, or strips of board or card, depending on the gap.

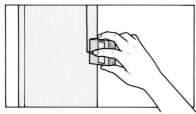

1 Scribe and cut the lining boards to fit flush with the front of the alcove, using a wood block and pencil to mark the profile of the back wall.

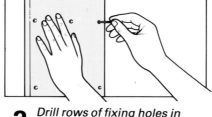

2 Drill rows of fixing holes in the boards at 450mm (18″) intervals, then offer up each board and mark where to drill and plug the wall.

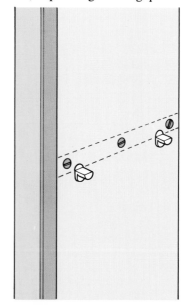

3 Hold a spirit level against the board as you screw it to the wall. Slip pieces of packing behind – resting them on the screws – to keep the board plumb.

4 Having lined the other side in the same way, hide any gaps between the boards and the wall with strips of panel moulding, pinned and glued to the edges.

With the lining boards in place, drill rows of holes for the plug-in supports at regular intervals. You can arrange for the shelf ends to hide the screw heads.

PUTTING UP TRACK SHELVES

Open track shelving systems are the perfect way to store things which don't need to be kept locked away and look good enough to be on show. The shelves are easy to fit, and you can adjust them as and when your storage needs change.

At the heart of any track system are the tracks themselves – long metal strips containing sets of holes at roughly 25mm (1″) intervals into which you lock the brackets.

Because of their length, tracks tend to be more stable than individual brackets. And since the track brackets' positions are already fixed, there's no tricky aligning to do – the only critical stages are fixing the first track vertical, and then getting the others level with it.

Although you can reset the bracket heights in a few minutes, in practice you'll probably find you set them once and then leave them that way. Even so, with the tracks already in place it's easy to add further shelves if you need them.

....Shopping List....

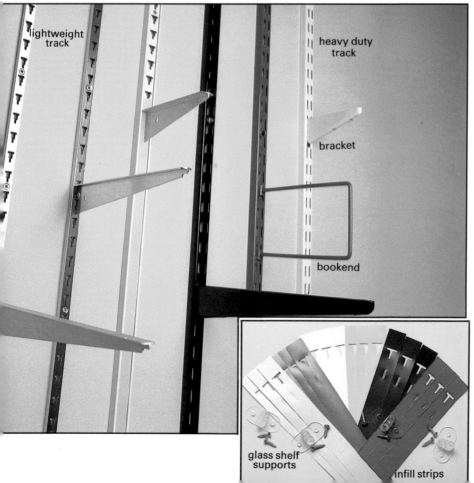

lightweight track

heavy duty track

bracket

bookend

glass shelf supports

infill strips

All systems include uprights and brackets in a range of lengths, but other accessories may also be available depending on the make. These include:
- Coloured infill strips to cover unused slots and match the uprights to your decor.
- Bookends.
- Glass shelf supports.
- Sloping brackets for display shelves.
- Panel brackets for fixing wallboards, etc.
- Cabinet brackets for fixing boxes and vertical panels to uprights.

Some manufacturers also offer a wide range of shelf sizes and finishes to suit their tracks, while others leave you to choose your own. Possible options include veneered chipboard (with a wood or plastic surface finish), blockboard and solid timber. The material you choose may affect the amount of support required (see overleaf).

Tools: Drill with masonry and wood bits, screwdriver, tape measure, spirit level (also a saw and try square if you have to cut shelves).

DESIGNING WITH STANDARD UNITS

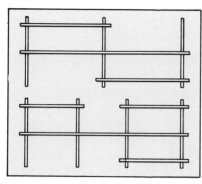

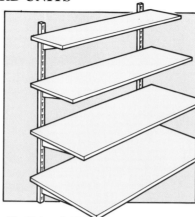

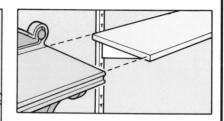

Shelf length Having three or more tracks allows you to fit shelves of different lengths, none of which need necessarily span the entire system.

This is particularly useful if you have to put a few tall items among objects that look best with the shelves closely spaced.

Shelf depth Fitting shelves of different depths makes it possible to store a wide range of items more efficiently within a small space. Always put the shelves in decreasing order of depth, from bottom to top.

Fixed levels If you want the shelving to line up with a feature of the room, such as a mantelpiece, you'll need to take extra care when marking the positions of the tracks.

The only reliable way to work out the final shelf level is to fit a bracket to a track and align it with the feature before you mark the screw holes – not forgetting to allow for the thickness of the shelf itself in your calculations.

WHAT TO FIX TO

On a solid masonry wall, fix the tracks by screwing through each of the fixing holes into drilled and plugged holes in the wall.

On a hollow timber-framed partition wall, you *must* screw the tracks to the solid timber framework itself. It is not sufficient to fix them to the hollow part of the wall using cavity wall fixings – the thin skin covering the wall will not be strong enough.

The tracks are flexible enough to cope with small irregularities in the wall, but if the surface is very uneven it's a good idea to fix battens to it first (see Problem Solver).

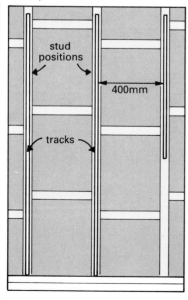

stud positions

400mm

tracks

Right Track systems aren't just for shelving; here one of the shelves doubles as a lightweight desk.

Left Using more than two tracks lets you position short runs of shelving at different heights.

HOW MANY SUPPORTS?

If you are fixing to a hollow wall, the track positions are governed by the position of the timber frame. You must screw to *each* stud – approximately 400mm (16″) intervals.

Otherwise, the maximum spacing is fixed by the material you are using for the shelving. The standard 15mm (⅝″) chipboard used as shelving material needs support at 600mm (24″) intervals to stop it bowing. But with very sturdy material, such as 25mm (1″) thick softwood or 19mm (¾″) blockboard, you can extend this to 900mm (3′).

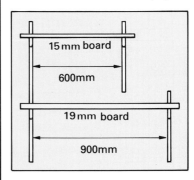

15 mm board
600mm
19 mm board
900mm

The brackets should either be the same depth as the shelves or a little less.

Remember, the longer the brackets, the *less* the amount of evenly distributed weight they will stand – 150mm (6″) brackets might carry well over 50kg (110lb), whereas 450mm (18″) brackets could be limited to as little as 15kg (35lb).

If you have to put heavy weights on a deep shelf, it's worth fitting tracks and brackets at more frequent intervals.

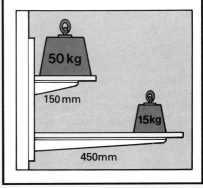

50 kg
150 mm
15 kg
450mm

Left Here, short lengths of track are used to create a streamlined run of shelves.

FIXING THE TRACKS

1 Mark the position of the top hole of the first track. If the shelf height is critical you will need to fit a bracket and align it first (see opposite).

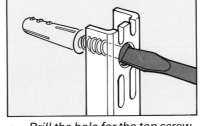

2 Drill the hole for the top screw and fix the track to the wall. Only partially tighten the screw, so that the track is left free to pivot on its fixing.

3 Use a spirit level to set the track vertically, then mark and drill the other holes. Fit the remaining screws, using packing pieces where necessary.

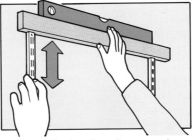

4 Use the level again to set the top of the second track at exactly the same height as the first. If you don't do this the shelves won't sit straight.

FIXING THE SHELVES

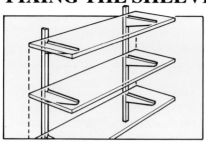

1 *Align the shelves so they overlap the brackets by the same amount on each side. Make sure, too, that the ends line up above one another.*

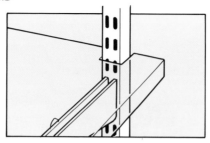

2 *If you want the shelves to fit right back against the wall, cut notches in them to accommodate the thickness of the tracks.*

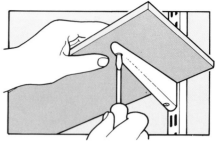

3 *Fit the brackets to the tracks, position the shelves and weight them, then mark the screw holes from underneath with a bradawl. Screw the brackets on.*

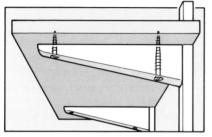

4 *With U-shaped brackets, the outer screw is shorter than the inner one. If you are using thin shelves, take care not to screw right through the boards.*

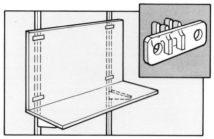

5 *Some systems have brackets for vertical panels. If yours doesn't, but you want to fit such panels, you can screw them to the shelves instead.*

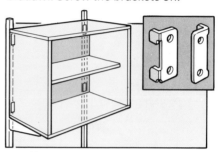

6 *If you want to include box units, these can either be home-made or adapted from basic self-assembly cabinets such as kitchen wall units.*

Trade tip

Strengthening shelves

❝ I find that a good way to stop thin shelves from bowing is to fix wood lipping along the edge. This also makes them look more substantial. A thin strip of softwood or ramin – about 50 × 12mm (2 × ½") – is usually ideal; fix it either to the front or back of the shelf. ❞

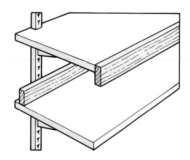
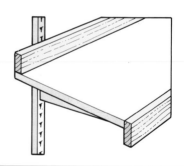

PROBLEM SOLVER

Uneven walls

Very few walls are perfectly flat or square, so when you screw the tracks in place make sure they don't bend because of irregularities in the surface.

Small bumps and hollows can be accommodated by inserting packing pieces of hardboard or cardboard behind the tracks as you drive in the screws.

If the walls are seriously out of square or in poor condition, it's better to screw 50 × 25mm (2 × 1") battens to the wall and then screw the tracks to these. This gives you more scope for packing behind the battens and lets you make the wall fixings where you like, rather than at points fixed by the tracks.

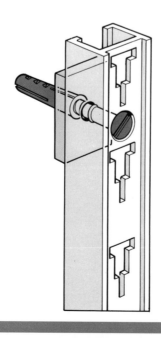
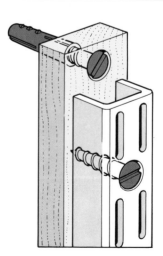

Fit packing pieces (left) to fill small hollows, but fit a batten (above) if the surface is poor.

FITTING GLASS SHELVING

Glass can be used with most types of shelf support and is an attractive alternative to more conventional shelving materials. The main reasons for using glass instead of wood are:
- Glass has a light, delicate appearance which doesn't overpower small objects and ornaments.
- It is easy to clean and doesn't stain, making it a practical choice for bathrooms and kitchens.
- It transmits light, so it can be used where solid shelves would cast unwanted shadows, such as in front of a mirror or around a window.

Glass also has disadvantages:
- It is brittle and broken glass can be dangerous, so glass shelves need good support and shouldn't be fitted within reach of small children.
- Heavy objects need thick glass shelves to provide adequate strength. As the shelves themselves are heavy, you need more supports than for an equivalent wooden shelf.

The main appeal of glass is its appearance, but it has practical advantages, too. In situations where a shelf could block the light, there is no other choice.

.... Shopping List....

As with any shelving, you must take into account the thickness of the shelf material and the amount of support it needs to suit the weight it has to carry.

Glass should be at least 6mm thick, depending on the load (see below). The normal choice is flat (float) clear glass, but other suitable types include coloured, patterned and wired glass – all of which can be used to decorative effect.
- 6mm glass is suitable for light loads if the shelves are supported every 400mm (16″).
- 10mm glass can be used for normal loads with brackets up to 700mm (28″) apart – reduce this to 500mm (20″) for books.

Get the glass cut to size by a glass merchant. All edges should be ground and polished smooth. Standard shelf widths are available pre-cut and finished.

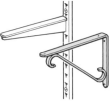

Brackets depend partly on the situation, but in general glass is heavy so use a medium/heavy duty system. The main options are:

Track systems which can be used either with special plastic retaining clips or self-adhesive glass fixing pads on the brackets.

Metal channels which grip the back of the shelves to give an unobtrusive fixing. These come in a range of colours and are suitable for 6mm glass only (a special insert is used to protect the glass from contact with the metal).

Shelf brackets are often unsuitable because the part of the bracket which is seen through the shelf looks infinished. A popular option is 'wrought iron' type brackets which look neat used in this way. Some pressed steel brackets can be fitted with special glass shelf clips which grip the shelf neatly.

Glass shelf brackets are commonly made for use in bathrooms. Most are designed to fit over the ends of a shelf which is cut to suit.

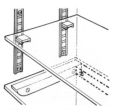

Alcove supports are an option where you are fitting shelves in a recess or a fitted cabinet.

Plug-in end supports include plastic plugs to fit into pre-drilled holes, or metal bookcase strips which screw to the sides ready to take clips at any height you wish.

Battens or metal angle screwed to sides and back of an alcove provide a means of giving continuous support for the shelves.

DESIGNING WITH GLASS SHELVES

ILLUMINATED SHELVING

Make use of transparent glass shelves in illuminated cabinets, where lights at the top or bottom can be arranged to shine right through. This is particularly effective when you are storing glassware or if the shelves nearest the light aren't cluttered but have only one or two objects on them.

Use downlighters or striplights to light up the cabinet. Low-voltage halogen downlighters are particularly good (although they are more expensive) as they are very small and generate less heat. The wiring too is smaller and therefore less conspicuous.

An easy way to house a downlighter is to fit it into a wooden panel the same size as a shelf. Fix this like a shelf, leaving clearance for the body of the light, and then box in the front to conceal the works.

LIGHTWEIGHT LOOKS

Use glass shelves as near-invisible supports for glassware and lightweight ornaments. They are particularly suitable for short spans in narrow alcoves or in cupboards with uprights at regular intervals.

Glass shelves can also be used to similar effect on flat walls, but here it is important to choose your supports carefully as many systems can look too heavy for the shelves. Two of the best options are lightweight tracks or the aluminium channel 'bracketless' system which grips the back edge of the shelf only.

If you choose separate brackets, delicate wrought iron types are particularly effective.

WINDOW SHELVES

Shelves in a window can be used to good effect to display ornamental glassware or to grow plants where they will receive plenty of natural light. There are also occasions where a window is the only practical place to put a shelf – for example, in a small bathroom where the washbasin is under a window.

If the window is in a shallow recess, treat it like a flat wall and support the shelves on brackets or tracks on either side. Where this leaves too large an unsupported span, fit a centre support by fixing a batten vertically across the frame.

Treat a deeply recessed window like an alcove, supporting the shelves on the inner face at both sides. If the span is too great, you must fit an intermediate bracket. Either fix it to a centre rail of the window (if there is one) or add a separate supporting batten.

ROOM DIVIDERS

A room divider or partial partition wall can be fitted with open glass shelves so that both rooms get the maximum light and share the storage area.

Plan the design to avoid having shelves at a low level where they are easily knocked into. In a partition, you can create 'windows' and span them with shelving; design a room divider so that it has low level cupboards or wooden shelves.

The easiest way to arrange the supports is to fit uprights in pairs. These can then be fitted with end supports by using bookcase strips or shelf plugs. You must obey the general rules about spacing the supports to suit the thickness of the glass and the weight of the things on the shelf.

FITTING GLASS SHELVES

Supports for glass shelves are fitted in much the same way as for any other shelf. However, it is even more important than usual to make sure that they are properly aligned – the shelf needs support across its whole width without undue flexing.

Some systems incorporate clips which prevent the glass from sliding on the brackets. Otherwise, if there is any risk at all of it being knocked, you should use self-adhesive retaining pads to hold it firmly in place on its supports.

To retain the glass on plain brackets, use double-sided self-adhesive pads. These also help to cushion it from contact with metal surfaces.

Trade tip

Using a dummy

6 With many support systems it often helps to line up the brackets by trying a shelf in place. To make it easier to do this and to simplify cutting the glass shelves to size, cut a dummy shelf from an offcut of chipboard or other suitable material and use this for your fitting experiments. 9

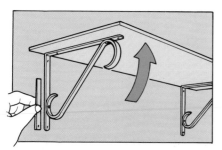

Align track and bracket systems carefully. Pack out behind the fixings if necessary to make sure that the shelf is fully supported and not twisted in any way.

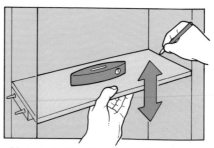

Alcove shelf battens must be carefully aligned. Fix one end first and align the second one by trying a shelf in place and marking along it.

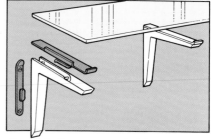

Special clips are needed for some brackets. Take care that these trap the edge of the glass without undue pressure which could cause splintering.

▋PROBLEM SOLVER▐

Polishing the edges

In most cases you can buy the glass ready cut and polished by the glass merchant. If you want to use a piece of glass which you have already, you can cut your own shelves with a glass cutter in the conventional way. But before use, you must also grind and polish the edges to prevent accidents.

This isn't very difficult to do, but it does take a little time. The easiest tool to use is an oilstone, but you can get by with a piece of wet or dry abrasive paper pinned to a block of wood. Start with a coarse abrasive and work down to fine.

Wear heavy gloves when handling the unpolished glass. Wet the stone (or paper) lightly and rub the edges of the glass, at an angle of about 45°. Use only downward strokes at this stage in case of splinters being pulled off the rough edge.

Rub down all the edges with the coarse abrasive until the sharp corners are removed, then switch to a medium abrasive. Wet this too and rub it along the edge to round off the ridges left by the first pass. Use this stone to take off the sharp corners.

Finish off with a fine abrasive, again used wet, running it along the edges at several angles until it produces a smooth curve.

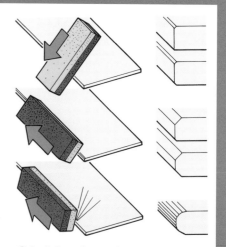

Grind the edges with progressively finer abrasive used wet. Work in the order shown to produce a smoothly rounded edge with a polished surface.

SPACE-SAVING STORAGE: CUPBOARDS

Equipping your home with ample cupboard space not only makes it easier to live in – it enhances its resale value too. But fully fitted kitchens and built-in wardrobes are only part of the story: you can do a lot simply by refitting the cupboards already there, and putting unused corners to better use.

Cupboard space to store items that aren't for show is an essential feature of modern living. The neater and tidier you are by habit, the more you are likely to need – but somehow no home ever seems to have quite enough!

Faced by the need for more cupboards, start by considering the various options:

Free-standing cupboards give you the freedom to rearrange storage from room to room as and when necessary, and to take it with you when you move. As well as buying new, you may be able to make use of inherited or secondhand wardrobes, sideboards and dressers.

The drawback is that unless individual cupboards fit the available spaces exactly, there is bound to be a certain amount of wasted space on either side and above the cupboard.

Modular systems (eg cube storage) which butt up together – and sometimes stack too – tend to be less wasteful of space. They are also a lot more flexible, so tend to make up in practicality for what they may lack in looks. Simple self-assembly

systems provide perfect storage-on-a-budget, especially for a first home.

Built-in units, usually sold flat-packed to assemble yourself, are a more sophisticated development of the modular principle. Many are designed specifically for kitchens, bedrooms or bathrooms, but there is no reason why you can't consider using them elsewhere.

Flat-pack or knock-down furniture of this type can usually be adapted to make good use of the available space, and offers a limited amount of scope for rearrangement. But don't bank on taking it with you if you move: as well as being hard to dismantle, the units are unlikely to come through transit unscathed in their knocked-down state.

Custom-built fitted cupboards are the ultimate in space-saving storage. Professional fitting is likely to be very expensive, but it is a relatively straightforward DIY task to put together a frame in softwood, and add standard size ready-made doors.

STORAGE CHECKLIST

■ On balance, how frequently do you like to move things around? If the answer is 'often', it is not a good idea to commit yourself too heavily to built-ins.

■ When considering built-ins, don't forget their effect on the room proportions and the amount of space left for walking around. It may pay you to draw a sketch plan indicating drawer and door opening swings.

■ For wall-mounted cupboards and built-in units, don't forget to check the wall construction: timber framed hollow walls tend to limit where you put things, since you must fix to the studs.

■ How likely are you to move? In this respect, totally built-in storage is likely to be a better investment than a system based on modular units; the first should look like 'part of the house', while the style and layout of the second may not be to everyone's taste.

Adapt existing furniture to make better use of the space: here (below left) an old cupboard has been fitted with sliding racks to make a useful china store.
Fitted bedroom furniture can be adapted to fit every nook and cranny – even sloping ceilings.

FINDING THE SPACE

With the options in mind, take a careful look at what has to be stored room-by-room – and also at the way it is stored at the moment. Empty spaces inside existing fitted cupboards and wardrobes suggest that you aren't making the best use of them. But before you add extra hardware to make the space more efficient, it's helpful to know exactly what's to be stored there. (It may be that some items can go completely, or be packed away in the loft or garage).

It's also important to consider the room as a whole when choosing storage. Try to position cupboards so that they complement, rather than detract from, any decorative mouldings or other original features. As far as finish is concerned, aim for a look which suits the character of the room and creates a balanced visual impact.

IN THE LIVING ROOM . . .

Most living rooms benefit from a combination of open shelves and cupboard storage, depending on how much there is to display.

■ Supplement alcove shelving with built-in cupboards at the base. If you make them 500–600mm (20–24") deep, they can be a convenient resting place for the TV or hi-fi.

■ Arrange modular systems along an entire wall, around a corner, or on either side of a window; shelving units help to break up a solid expanse of cupboard doors.

■ Glass-fronted cupboards provide display storage and keep out dust at the same time.

■ In a combined living/dining room, divide the areas with free-standing cupboards; for example, position a sideboard back to back with a sofa.

■ Replace side tables beside sofas and armchairs with small free-standing cupboards for holding magazines or odds and ends.

Modular systems (main picture) often combine cupboards and shelves. Glass fronted cupboards are practical, and less intrusive than solid doors.
Replace side tables (inset) with cupboards for magazines and so on.

IN THE KITCHEN . . .

Even if you don't possess the luxury of row upon row of neatly fitted cupboards, you can at least ensure you make the best use of the space you have.

■ Moving out appliances such as a freezer or washing machine can free valuable cupboard space. Alternative sites include the garage, or under the stairs.

■ Take advantage of modern fitted kitchen accessories – wire baskets, carousels and so on – to refit an old built-in cupboard or larder.

■ Don't forget that hanging items such as brooms or pans can free usable space in a tall cupboard.

■ Consider replacing a kitchen table with a breakfast bar containing extra cupboards; or swap conventional chairs for built-in bench seating with lift-up lids and sliding doors below – ideal for storing heavy items.

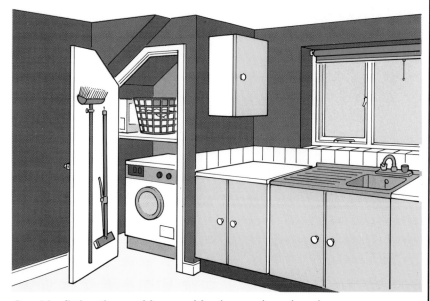

Consider fitting the washing machine in a cupboard, and make maximum use of space with extra shelves and hooks.

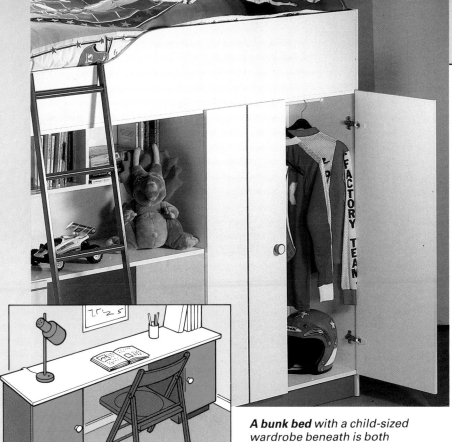

IN CHILDRENS' ROOMS . . .

The way you organize storage here depends on the age of the child. Because their needs change so rapidly, it is a good idea to keep things as flexible as possible by using free-standing cupboards or adjustable shelves.

■ For the first year, a simple, low-level cupboard or chest of drawers (also doubling as a changing surface) should meet most storage needs. A washbasin and vanity unit are likely to be more useful than a large cupboard.

■ After a couple of years, you will probably need a small wardrobe, or hanging space fitted beneath a shelf and screened with a curtain rather than conventional doors.

■ School-age children need plenty of floor space, so consider raising the bed and fitting storage underneath. There are many ready-made units with wardrobes, shelves or even desks below them to maximize the use of space.

■ Teenagers need worktop space as well as storage. A tabletop fitted between a pair of cupboards or chests of drawers could provide the ideal compromise.

A bunk bed with a child-sized wardrobe beneath is both practical and popular with youngsters (4 years upwards). In a teenage study cupboards can be used to support a desktop

IN THE BEDROOM . . .

Bedrooms may well provide you with useful space for storing spare linen and suitcases, plus items you don't use regularly such as a sewing machine or typewriter. Of course, clothes will take up the bulk of the space.

■ Wardrobes and fitted cupboards should be at least 600mm (2') deep for conventional clothes hanging, and will need building out if located in a shallow recess. The alternative is to hang clothes flat-on, in which case too much depth is a positive disadvantage.

■ Other possible sites for built-in cupboards are either side of a large window, or beside and above the bed.

■ Take cupboards right up to ceiling height where possible, and use the top part for storing spare linen, or any clothes which are out of season, to save space in the lower areas.

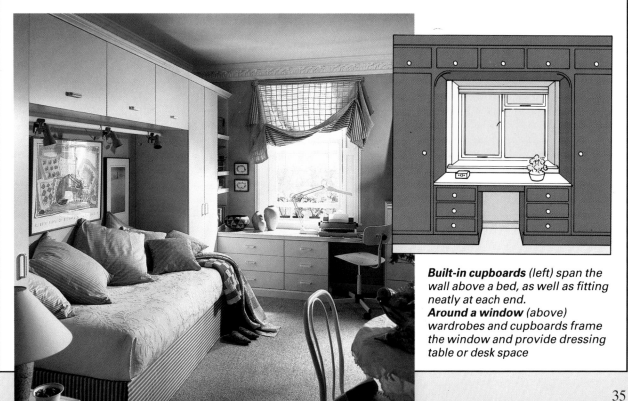

Built-in cupboards (left) span the wall above a bed, as well as fitting neatly at each end.
Around a window (above) wardrobes and cupboards frame the window and provide dressing table or desk space

IN THE BATHROOM . . .

Fully fitted bathrooms are the latest arrival on the luxury fitted unit scene, but there are plenty of other ways to make use of what is often a rather cramped space.

■ Pedestal basins waste space; consider replacement with a cupboard containing an inset basin.

■ The wall above the WC is another 'dead area': either fit a wall-hung cabinet, or box in the cistern with cupboards up to ceiling height.

■ A lockable medicine cupboard is essential in family homes, but don't restrict yourself to ready-made ones (which are often impractical in size). You could lock medicines in a box,

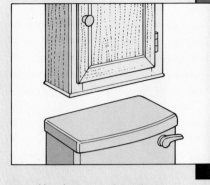

stored in a larger cupboard.

■ Boxed-in baths can provide extra storage for cleaning materials and odds and ends: simply fit a new panel with magnetic catches.

Make use of space under the basin and above the shower with simple, DIY cupboards and louvre doors. The wall above the cistern (left) may provide space for a cabinet.

MAKING THE MOST OF IT

Once you have planned all the cupboards you think you need, give another thought to the space inside them. Extra shelves, hooks and other arrangements may be useful. You may find you can fit extra cupboards above existing ones. And bifold or concertina doors could enable you to fit cupboards where you didn't think there was space because of the opening swing of conventional doors.

Look to the ceiling to 'top up' the storage space provided by an existing built-in cupboard. If fitting new modular units, try kitchen cupboard ranges (which usually offer more choice) for a series of units to fit the space. Many glass-fronted kitchen units also look equally at home in a living room.

Illuminate deep cupboards to stop the clutter piling up. There are fluorescent and tungsten strip or festoon fittings specially made for cupboards.

Think of your back: store the heaviest items at waist level, so that you can lift them without bending or stretching.

The back of a door can be fitted with hooks or rails to hold long thin items. A boon for a bedroom is the shoe tidy.

Door choice can make all the difference where space is tight. Sliding doors maximize floor space, but restrict access. Concertina or bifold doors are often a good compromise.

Shelves aren't necessarily the best choice. The alternatives include kit drawers or wire/plastic baskets on runners mounted underneath.

HALLS AND LANDINGS

Halls and landings can provide unexpected storage space. Besides storage for outside clothes and cleaning equipment, you may be able to find space for DIY and other hobby materials.

■ Look back at the front door: there's often space above and beside it for fitted cupboards.

■ The space under the stairs can be used for waist-level cupboards, or opened out – as desk space for example.

■ Replace a single cupboard door under the stairs with a series of doors, to give better access. Partitions and shelves inside the cupboard may help too.

■ On landings, or the return wall above the stairs, high wall-mounted cupboards could provide long-term storage space.

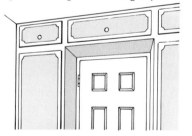

High level and narrow, upright cupboards fit neatly around a front door in the hallway.

Good access can make better use of space: extra doors have been fitted under these stairs.

BUILT-IN CUPBOARDS

Built-in cupboards are the neatest solution to household storage problems. Unlike free-standing furniture, they can be planned to make the best use of the available space, and you can ensure that they don't obstruct the rest of the room. And although you can't take them with you if you move, most potential purchasers see plenty of built-in cupboards as a real asset.

One way to provide built-in cupboard space is to buy modular furniture such as kitchen or bedroom units. But although this is likely to be the easiest option, it may not always be the best. If you have an awkward space (or it simply doesn't fit the modular unit size very well) you may find that the units fill it little better than free-standing furniture. Modular units can also work out fairly expensive, simply because the makers have to ensure that they are structurally sound regardless of where they are fitted or what is on each side.

Building your own furniture is rather more complicated, but can offer some significant advantages.

First of all, you can ensure that things fit properly. For example, if you have a space which is 1050mm wide, you can build a unit this size rather than having to adapt a stan-

Traditional styling suits living room alcoves.

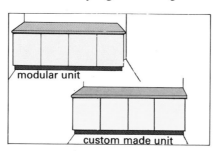

Custom designed built-in furniture can be made to fit an awkward space perfectly – unlike modular furniture which is restricted to set sizes.

dard unit which is probably 900 or 1000mm wide (or use a combination of 500 and 600mm wide ones).

Secondly, you can save on materials by making more use of the walls themselves (or adjacent cupboards) as supports.

Thirdly, you can produce furniture which simply isn't available any other way. For example, you can make shallow cupboards that fit a shallow alcove perfectly, rather than using deeper standard ones which would project awkwardly.

Types of built-in furniture
There are two basic ways to make built-in furniture:

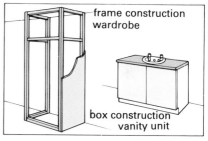

Box furniture is easy to make and most furniture is now built this way. Frame furniture is more complicated but lighter and more economical on materials.

Framed furniture uses battens as the main structural supports, and in many cases – for example, alcove shelving – the battens can be fixed directly to the walls. Any of the framework left exposed can then be clad with non-structural panelling, which also serves to brace it.

Box furniture uses panels of sheet material (eg chipboard) as the main structural supports; most modern self-assembly units are built this way.

In practice, you may find it is best to use a combination of methods. On the following pages are a number of basic designs which can be adapted to many situations.

DESIGNING BUILT-IN FURNITURE

There are no hard-and-fast rules for desgining built-in furniture: by its very nature, each piece should be made to suit the situation. This means taking a flexible attitude, and adapting basic design principles as you go.

Start by measuring up the room and drawing a scale plan. This should show all the critical dimensions, and you may find you need to draw two plans (one to show the floor and another showing the walls) to include enough detail. Mark in any fixed points such as electrical sockets and water pipes.

Next draw a rough sketch of the furniture you have in mind. There are two things which you should consider right from the start. First of all, try to stick to the standard dimensions given in the table on the right when it comes to things like worktop height and so on. If you are in doubt about overall sizes, measure some

finished furniture as a starting point.

Secondly, bear in mind the available sizes of the materials you plan to use. For example, faced chipboard comes in 300 and 375mm (12 and 15″) widths. Making a unit 325mm (13″) deep means trimming down the wider boards (unless you go up to a larger sheet and can cut several strips from it with less waste). Unless there is an over-riding reason for sticking to a specific non-standard dimension, use standard boards for ease of work and economy. Similarly, work to standard lengths as far as possible.

Finally, it is worth taking advantage of ready made accessories wherever possible – to save time and to ensure a good finish.
■ Standard ready made doors and drawer fronts can save hours of work. See the following construction plans for more details.
■ Drawers are rarely worth con-

structing from scratch, since drawer kits are simple, reasonably cheap and very efficient. These are covered in a separate chapter.

When you have roughed out the design to your satisfaction, transfer it accurately to the scale plan. This forms both the basis of your shopping list and a guide to construction.

STANDARD DIMENSIONS

Worktop depth	600mm
Worktop/sink height	900mm
Worktop to-wall unit gap	450mm
Dressing table height	600–800mm
Wardrobe depth	500–600mm
Seating height	400–450mm
Dining table height	700–750mm
Washbasin height	700mm
Chest of drawers depth	400–450mm
Shelf supports	600–750mm apart

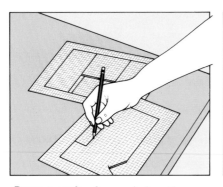

Draw a scale plan and elevation of the room showing all the critical dimensions and the position of any fixed points like sockets and pipes.

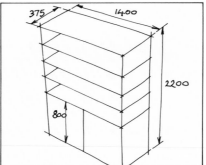

Sketch out your furniture design, roughly indicate overall height and depth. Choose the overall dimensions to suit the materials and fittings you are using.

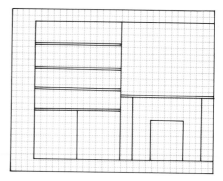

Adapt your drawing to suit the scale plan and then draw it on the plan accurately to scale. This becomes your shopping list and cutting plan.

....Shopping List....

Sheet materials The main material for low-cost box furniture is *faced* or *veneered* 16mm (⅝″) *chipboard*. This comes in 2240×1220mm (8×4′) sheets and a variety of board widths and lengths.

Alternatives for painting include *MDF* and *blockboard*. Blockboard is very strong and comes in a variety of several thicknesses, is easy to work, stable and easy to finish. *Veneered blockboard* can be used for varnished wood furniture. Both materials come in standard 2240×1220mm (8×4′) sheets.

Where you are panelling over a timber frame, the sheet material is not structural. *Hardboard* may be adequate, although it flexes easily and may 'drum'; it is often used to make furniture backs. Otherwise

use *thin plywood* . You can even use *plasterboard* for furniture which forms the corner of a room, providing the edges are covered and it does not have to take a load.

Other timber *Planed softwood battens* are the stock solution for built-in furniture. 50×25mm (2×1″) is adequate for most jobs.

Softwood mouldings are worth investigating as solutions to design or decor problems. They are particularly useful for concealing exposed edges, or to break up large expanses of flat panelling.

Doors and drawers Blank *door and drawer fronts* come in various styles in a small range of sizes. Common examples are:
■ Widths of 300, 375, 450, 600, 675, and 750mm.

■ Heights of 450, 600, 750, 900, 1200, 1500, 1650, 1800 and 2000mm.
(There may be some variation in the measurement depending on whether they are basically Imperial or metric sizes). Home made doors and drawer fronts can be any size you wish.

Fixings *PVA adhesive, chipboard screws* in various sizes and *panel pins* should cope with most jobs; buy plenty, as it is almost impossible to plan exact needs in advance. It is also worth buying *brackets* or *block joints* in bulk for the same reason.

Fittings *Drawer kits, hinges, knobs* and other fittings can be estimated fairly accurately. DIY superstores often sell such items in bulk.

ADAPTABLE LIVING ROOM UNITS

These units can be used as either a sideboard/dresser or bookcase/entertainments centre by making small modifications to the design and construction. It's also easy to change the appearance to suit different furnishing styles by applying mouldings and choosing different doors.

The construction is straightforward and is intended for use either in an alcove or in a corner – although it could easily be extended right across a room. Essentially, there are two parts; a base unit with worktop and a series of shelves above.

In an alcove, the shelves can be entirely supported on the wall, but where the unit is built into a corner you need to fit an end panel; in this case fit one against the wall too, for the sake of symmetry.

Making the doors

You can either use standard ready made doors which come in a lmited range of sizes, or make your own to fit. Ready made doors guarantee a good finish, but you are likely to have to panel-in gaps in the course of adapting them to fit the space.

Home-made doors can be made simply by using panels of faced or veneered chipboard, or blockboard edged with lipping. If you want a painted finish, MDF is the best choice. All these have a flat, stark appearance which is fine in modern rooms but not so good for period ones. If necessary, give the surface a panelled look by gluing on mouldings.

Finishing touches

There are two main ways to modify the style of the cupboards:

■ Choose materials with either a painted or natural wood finish in mind. If you are painting, use MDF, blockboard or a veneered chipboard; for a natural wood look use solid wood, veneered chipboard or veneered blockboard with matching lipping.

■ Pick mouldings to match other fittings in the room – the key to a real 'built-in' style. Trim the top with a cornice to match the coving in the room, and use architraves and cupboard door mouldings to match those on the other doors. You could also continue the skirting around the plinth, and run any picture rail across the unit at the same height.

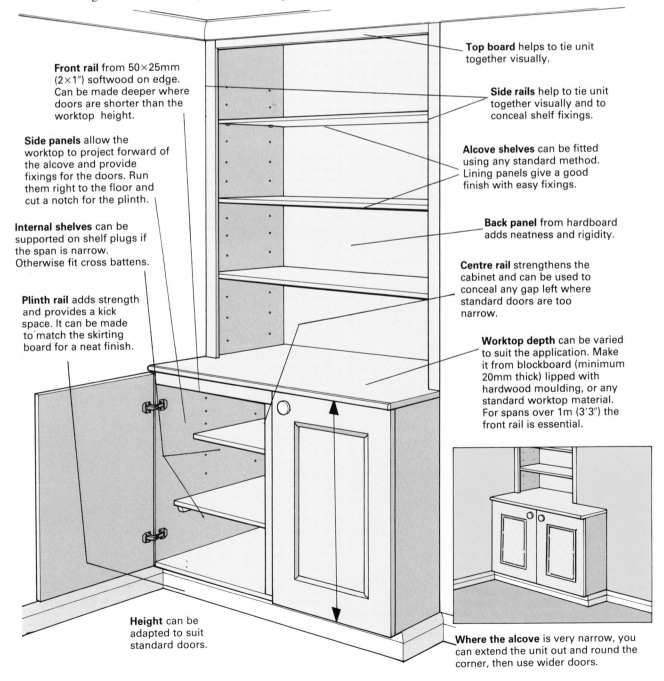

Front rail from 50×25mm (2×1") softwood on edge. Can be made deeper where doors are shorter than the worktop height.

Side panels allow the worktop to project forward of the alcove and provide fixings for the doors. Run them right to the floor and cut a notch for the plinth.

Internal shelves can be supported on shelf plugs if the span is narrow. Otherwise fit cross battens.

Plinth rail adds strength and provides a kick space. It can be made to match the skirting board for a neat finish.

Top board helps to tie unit together visually.

Side rails help to tie unit together visually and to conceal shelf fixings.

Alcove shelves can be fitted using any standard method. Lining panels give a good finish with easy fixings.

Back panel from hardboard adds neatness and rigidity.

Centre rail strengthens the cabinet and can be used to conceal any gap left where standard doors are too narrow.

Worktop depth can be varied to suit the application. Make it from blockboard (minimum 20mm thick) lipped with hardwood moulding, or any standard worktop material. For spans over 1m (3'3") the front rail is essential.

Height can be adapted to suit standard doors.

Where the alcove is very narrow, you can extend the unit out and round the corner, then use wider doors.

39

BASIC KITCHEN UNITS

Kitchen units can be made to suit awkward locations far more efficiently than standard self-assembly units. In general it makes sense to use similar construction methods, and where standard units are being used elsewhere in the kitchen it's a good idea to copy them.

The main reasons for making your own units are where standard ones don't fit a given width very well, or where you want to take top units right up to the ceiling.

All the fittings are easily obtainable from DIY superstores, and are fairly easy to use – although you need to buy a special hinge-boring bit to fit the type of hinges used on kitchen cupboard doors.

Door options

Doors are the major problem with home made kitchen units. If you want plain white flush doors, these are simple to make from sheets of coated chipboard (and you may also find this in a range of colours).

Where you are trying to match existing units, you really have no option but to use identical doors, bought as spares from the unit suppliers. This means that you have to work around standard sizes – which to some extent defeats the object of making your own units in the first place. However, even if you have to panel out the cupboard to suit the doors, you still have the internal space which is not available if you use smaller units.

Standard doors may also be the best option if you want something more interesting than a plain panel. There is no need to stick to kitchen unit doors; ready made cupboard doors are widely available in a range of sizes and can be varnished or painted as you choose.

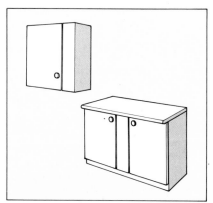

Options for adapting standard doors to fit all involve packing out the sides with extra strips, leaving the internal size unaltered. Don't do this on the hinge side, since the mounting plates need to be screwed to a flat panel.

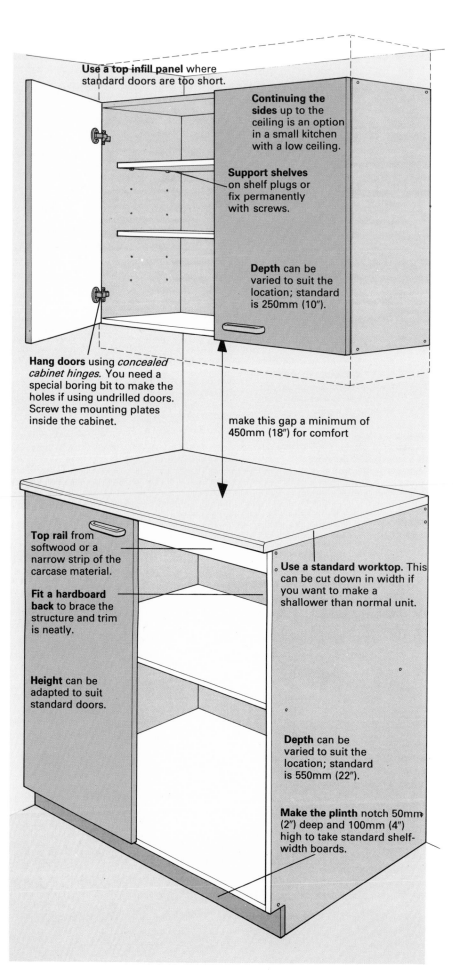

Use a top infill panel where standard doors are too short.

Continuing the sides up to the ceiling is an option in a small kitchen with a low ceiling.

Support shelves on shelf plugs or fix permanently with screws.

Depth can be varied to suit the location; standard is 250mm (10″).

Hang doors using *concealed cabinet hinges*. You need a special boring bit to make the holes if using undrilled doors. Screw the mounting plates inside the cabinet.

make this gap a minimum of 450mm (18″) for comfort

Top rail from softwood or a narrow strip of the carcase material.

Fit a hardboard back to brace the structure and trim is neatly.

Height can be adapted to suit standard doors.

Use a standard worktop. This can be cut down in width if you want to make a shallower than normal unit.

Depth can be varied to suit the location; standard is 550mm (22″).

Make the plinth notch 50mm (2″) deep and 100mm (4″) high to take standard shelf-width boards.

BUILDING-IN WARDROBES

Built-in wardrobes are easily put together using a combination of box and frame construction techniques. Alternatively, you can partition off the end or corner of a room and fit sliding doors.

However, in a small bedroom, it may not be worth going to the trouble of making the basic wardrobe – and a cheaper option may be to adapt a low-cost self-assembly unit. The dimensions of things like hanging space tend to be fairly fixed anyway, and it is rarely necessary to make the basic box fit a particular space with any degree of accuracy.

Whether you make the wardrobe from scratch or adapt an existing unit, the trick is to use the dressing table part to adjust it to fit the room exactly. Gaps can then simply be filled in by using mouldings – a theme which can be continued across the doors and so on.

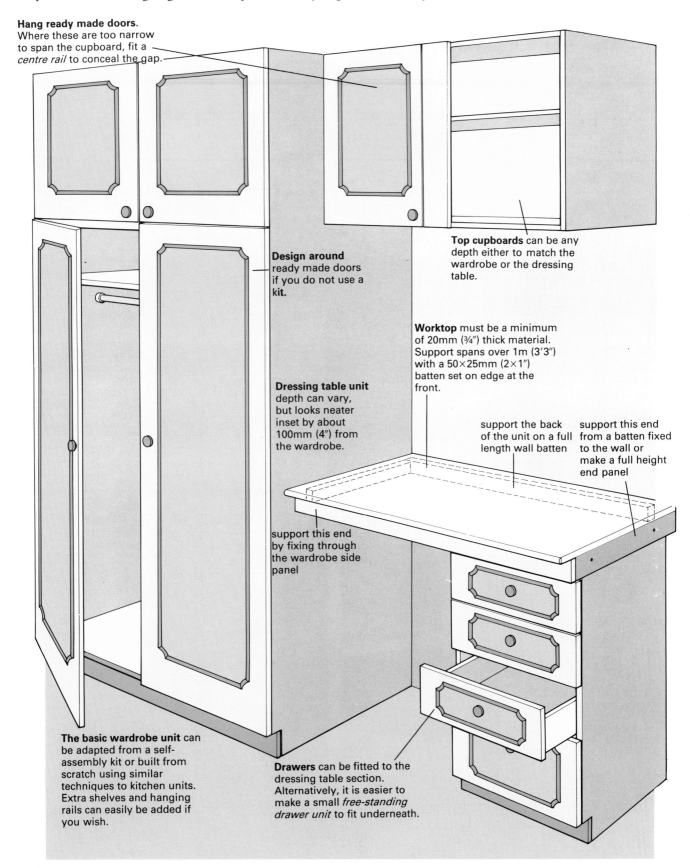

Hang ready made doors. Where these are too narrow to span the cupboard, fit a *centre rail* to conceal the gap.

Design around ready made doors if you do not use a kit.

Top cupboards can be any depth either to match the wardrobe or the dressing table.

Worktop must be a minimum of 20mm (¾″) thick material. Support spans over 1m (3′3″) with a 50×25mm (2×1″) batten set on edge at the front.

Dressing table unit depth can vary, but looks neater inset by about 100mm (4″) from the wardrobe.

support the back of the unit on a full length wall batten

support this end from a batten fixed to the wall or make a full height end panel

support this end by fixing through the wardrobe side panel

The basic wardrobe unit can be adapted from a self-assembly kit or built from scratch using similar techniques to kitchen units. Extra shelves and hanging rails can easily be added if you wish.

Drawers can be fitted to the dressing table section. Alternatively, it is easier to make a small *free-standing drawer unit* to fit underneath.

41

AIRING CUPBOARD

Airing cupboards need to run from floor to ceiling. This makes frame construction the natural choice; it is lighter than solid panels and you aren't restricted by the size of standard boards.

The hot water cylinder will normally be close to a corner, so all you have to do is to frame one side and hang doors across the other. You'll gain useful space by rerouting any intrusive pipes to run down walls.

Louvre doors are normally the best choice since they provide natural ventilation. If you use solid doors, you should fit vent panels to the top and bottom of the unit.

Planning points

■ Choose your doors first and work round their dimensions. Make sure there is room for them to swing.
■ Choose the cladding material – if this comes in sheets smaller than the height of the cupboard you must arrange for the joint to fall over a supporting batten. Suitable materials include plywood, hardboard, or plasterboard (so long as the exposed front edge is protected with a lipping).
■ Make sure you will have easy access to any gatevalves controlling the flow of water to the cylinder, and to the thermostat or switch for an immersion heater.

Construction details

■ Fix the wall battens first, ensuring they are accurately horizontal and vertical.
■ Assemble the side frame.
■ Use a door to measure where the side frame needs to be positioned.
■ Fix the frame to walls, floor and ceiling, making sure the door post is vertical (check from side to side and back to front, too).
■ Fix cross battens and a plinth.
■ Install the shelves.
■ Cover the frame with panelling.
■ Hang the doors.

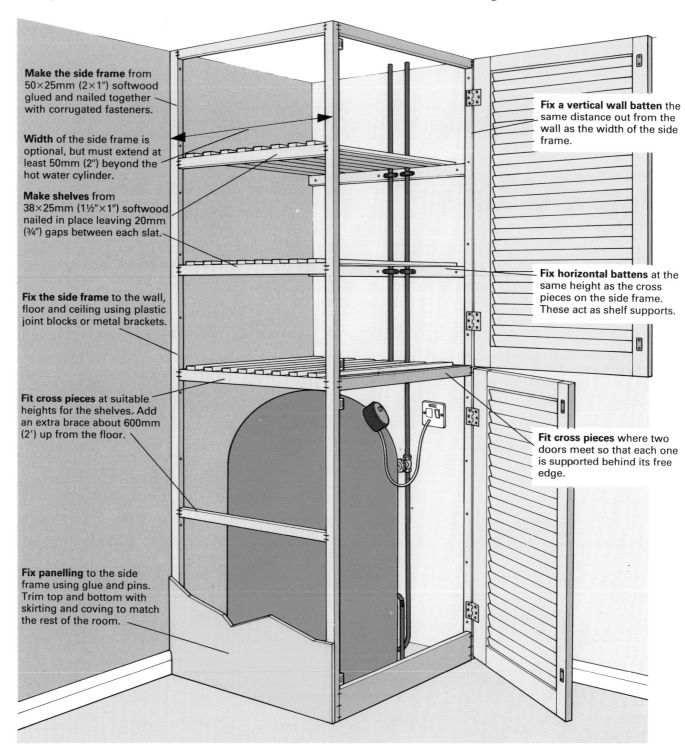

Make the side frame from 50×25mm (2×1″) softwood glued and nailed together with corrugated fasteners.

Width of the side frame is optional, but must extend at least 50mm (2″) beyond the hot water cylinder.

Make shelves from 38×25mm (1½″×1″) softwood nailed in place leaving 20mm (¾″) gaps between each slat.

Fix the side frame to the wall, floor and ceiling using plastic joint blocks or metal brackets.

Fit cross pieces at suitable heights for the shelves. Add an extra brace about 600mm (2′) up from the floor.

Fix panelling to the side frame using glue and pins. Trim top and bottom with skirting and coving to match the rest of the room.

Fix a vertical wall batten the same distance out from the wall as the width of the side frame.

Fix horizontal battens at the same height as the cross pieces on the side frame. These act as shelf supports.

Fit cross pieces where two doors meet so that each one is supported behind its free edge.

MAKING KIT DRAWERS

In traditional furniture making, drawers were always one of the most difficult things to construct, as they were made from thin wood held together by dozens of dovetail joints. Fortunately for modern DIY furniture makers, the advent of kit drawer systems has changed all that.

Plastic kit drawers are similar to the ones used in the majority of kitchen units and other flat-pack furniture. Most come in white, but beige is available in some ranges.

One type comes as a complete moulding ready to take your choice of front (you may need to fit your own base panel, too). These are made in standard cupboard unit sizes. The other version consists of pre-formed plastic sections which can be cut to any length and clipped together around a base panel.

In both caes, the drawer sides are fomed to fit either simple plastic glides or fully extending runners of the type used in better-quality ready-made furniture.

Accessories are also available to match most systems. These may include extension rails for use where a deeper drawer is required, or cutlery inserts for kitchens.

Plastic kit drawers *guarantee efficient operation and clean looks. Assembly should take a matter of minutes, leaving you to fit your choice of front panel.*

DRAWER FRONT OPTIONS

Drawer fronts can be made in several ways to suit different furniture:

Option 1 is to buy ready made blank fronts from a standard furniture range. This is the most expensive option and does not give much flexibility over their dimensions. However, you are likely to get a good finish for very little effort.

Option 2 is to make your own. There are various choices:

■ Coated or veneered chipboard can be cut to width and length. Edge with matching iron-on edging strip.

■ Softwood boards can be sawn to length and planed to width if necessary. Varnish or paint.

■ 'Panelled' drawer fronts can be made by cutting four sections of moulding and mitring the corners. Assemble these into a frame and glue onto a plywood or softwood front.

With some kits the drawer front supports one edge of the base. You may find that a channel section is provided which fits to the front and slots over the base. If not, you must either cut a slot in the front (tricky unless you possess a router) or support it from below with a moulding (see Problem Solver, page 45).

Sizes

If the front fits over the sides of the cabinet, it should be flush with them. If it fits inside the sides of the cabinet, allow at least 2mm (1/16") clearance each side – so make the drawer front about 4mm (1/8") smaller than the opening. Some drawer kits allow the front position to be adjusted.

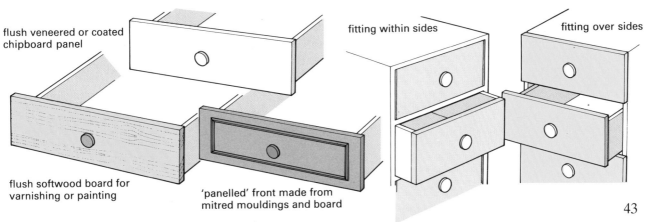

flush veneered or coated chipboard panel

fitting within sides

fitting over sides

flush softwood board for varnishing or painting

'panelled' front made from mitred mouldings and board

....Shopping List....

Moulded drawers are commonly available to fit into units 300, 400, 500 and 600mm wide (allowing for the thickness of sides made from 15, 16, or 18mm thick materials). In each case the cabinet must be more than 490mm deep. There are also *shallow depth* versions to suit cabinets down to 275mm deep, but these are normally only made in the 500mm width.

The standard height of the sides is 85mm, but you can buy extension rails to increase this to 140mm.

Some patterns come as a complete box incorporating a moulded-in base (*one-piece drawers*). With others, you have to assemble the sides and back, then slide a hardboard or plywood panel in. Plastic fronts are available for use where these are fitted inside a cabinet – eg as internal drawers in a wardrobe.

Self-assembly kits come in various forms. You may find *side profiles* made in continuous lengths which you cut to size as you wish. Some suppliers operate a cutting service, so you order to suit the size of the finished drawer. There are also ready made kits in standard sizes.

In each case you need special *corner joints*. Depending on the system, these may be a simple push-fit, they may fix with adhesive, or they may lock into notches cut in the profile. In the latter case, you need to make use of a cutting service, because a special tool is needed to form the notches. If you are using false drawer fronts (see page 46) you need four corners. If you are joining the profiles directly to the drawer front, you only need two corners, but also need a pair of *frontplates*.

Drawer bases are needed in both cases. Use 3mm hardboard or plywood – faced or unfaced as you prefer. To secure them to a drawer front, you may need a *fixing channel*, but this depends on the design.

Runners come in various lengths from 300 to 500mm. Plain runners (also called *glides*) can be shortened if necessary. Roller runners cannot normally be cut down. Ready made drawers normally need special runners, which may vary to suit the thickness of the cabinet sides.

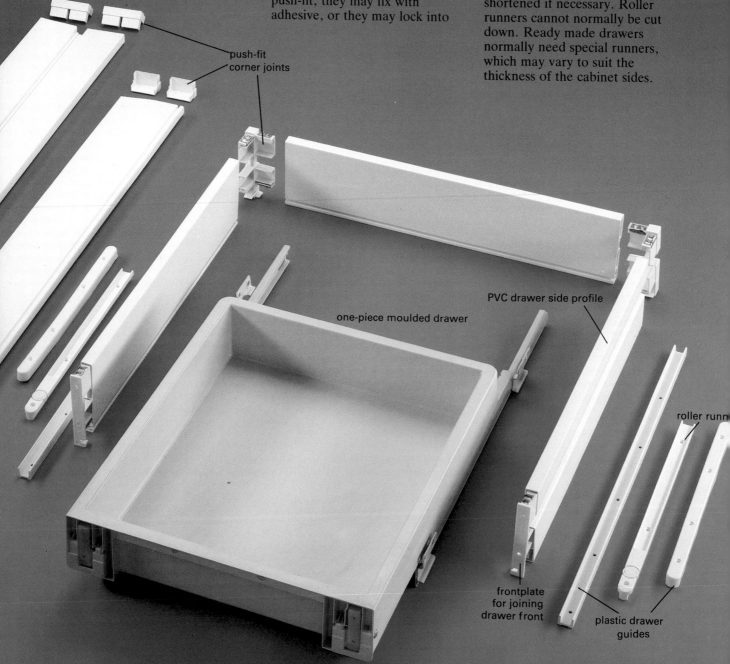

push-fit corner joints

one-piece moulded drawer

PVC drawer side profile

roller runn

frontplate for joining drawer front

plastic drawer guides

FITTING READY MADE DRAWERS

Ready made one-piece drawers can be made up in minutes. It takes a little longer if you need to assemble the sides and back.

One-piece drawers Turn the box over and press in the runner fixing clips; note that one is left and one is right handed. With the roller at the rear of the drawer, snap the drawer part of the runner mechanism into the box. Measure up the cabinet carefully and position the other halves of the runners inside at a corresponding height. Make sure they are level and then screw in place

setting them back very slightly.

Screw the front fixing brackets to the drawer front; these too are left and right handed. The correct spacing depends on the width of the drawer and is given in the instructions. The front may need to project above or below the base.

Push the drawer front into place. A screw is used to lock it in place; this also allows up to 3mm adjustment in any direction so you can position the front accurately to align with a run of cabinets.

Self-assembly drawers Press the

sides and back sections together. Cut a base from 3mm (⅛") hardboard and slide it into the base grooves; the correct dimensions should be given in the kit and are designed to leave it slightly projecting to fit a groove in the front.

Fit front brackets to the drawer front and press home. There is no method of adjustment with this system so measure very carefully.

Fit the roller mechanism to the grooves in the sides, then screw the runners to the cabinet, setting them back slightly from the front.

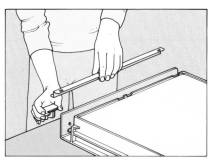

1 *One-piece drawers* have separate runners. Fit these to the underside of the box using the special clips supplied for each side.

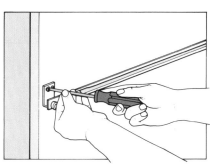

2 *Screw the other half of the runner mechanism to the inside of the cabinet taking care to fix it level and at the right height. Inset slightly from the front.*

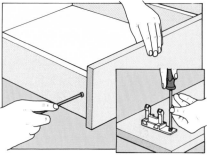

3 *Screw the fixing brackets to the drawer front after measuring carefully. Push into place and adjust if necessary using the screws provided.*

Trade tip

Check the position

❝Although the makers will give accurate specifications for positioning the drawer front on the box, it is fairly easy to miscalculate this. It's worth double checking your measurements by holding the drawer front against the box and seeing whether it looks correct in place in the cabinet. ❞

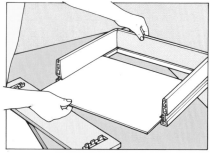

1 *Self-assembly kits* just snap together. Slide the base into place in the grooves, then screw the fixing brackets to the drawer front and push into the sides.

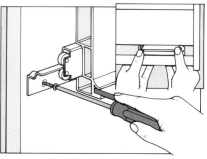

2 *Fit the roller mechanism into the grooves in each side. Then screw the metal runner sections to the cabinet, set back a little from the front edge.*

▌ PROBLEM SOLVER ▌

Support the base

Where the base is not supported by the plastic mouldings at the front, there are three options:
- Channel a groove in the front using a router. Leave the base projecting by about 6mm (¼").
- Fit a grooved fixing channel to the front and cut the base flush (if no special channel is available, adapt a sliding door channel or similar moulding).
- Cut the base flush and glue a strip of quadrant moulding underneath to support the edge.

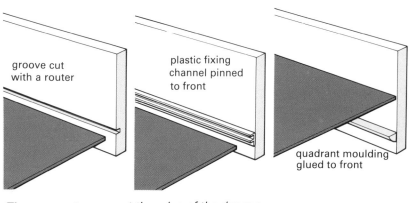

groove cut with a router

plastic fixing channel pinned to front

quadrant moulding glued to front

Three ways to support the edge of the drawer base in a three-sided kit system.

SELF-ASSEMBLY DRAWERS

Kit drawers can be made in two ways:

Option 1: four sided drawers. Assemble four side profiles and corner pieces around a base panel to make a complete box. Then attach this to a false drawer front.

Option 2: three sided drawer. Assemble three side profiles in a 'U' shape using two corner pieces. Fit a base and attach the front directly to the ends of the side profiles. This saves on materials and makes slightly more drawer space as well as looking neater. However, you do need to support the front of the base against the drawer front (see Problem Solver, page 45).

Measuring up

If the supplier cuts the profiles for you, all you need to do it to specify the size of the cabinet and whether you want the drawer front to fit inside the cabinet or overlapping the sides. If you are cutting your own parts, you need to do some careful calculations as shown on the right. Mark the profiles using a try-square and cut them carefully with a fine-toothed saw (eg a tenon saw).

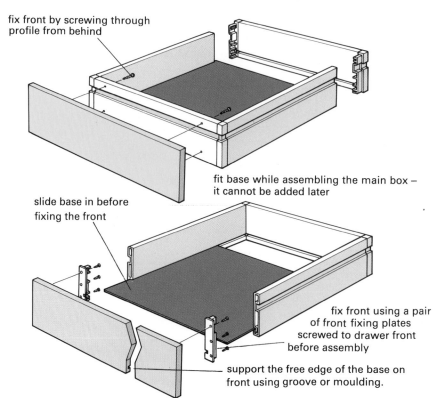

fix front by screwing through profile from behind

fit base while assembling the main box – it cannot be added later

slide base in before fixing the front

fix front using a pair of front fixing plates screwed to drawer front before assembly

support the free edge of the base on front using groove or moulding.

A four sided drawer is strong and easy to make, but the extra section takes up space inside.

A three sided drawer is more complicated. The front fixing brackets need to be carefully positioned and the front must also provide support for the base.

WORKING OUT SIZES

Use this method to calculate how long to make the sides and front/back profiles of the drawer. Measure dimensions (A), (B) and (C) as right. Then do these calculations:

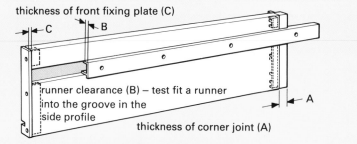

thickness of front fixing plate (C)

runner clearance (B) – test fit a runner into the groove in the side profile

thickness of corner joint (A)

Check these measurements before working out how long to cut the various sections of your drawer.

Width

■ Measure the opening from side to side.
■ Deduct twice the width of a corner joint (A).
■ Deduct twice the runner clearance (B).
■ Deduct 3mm to allow a small fitting clearance.

Four sided drawer sides

■ Measure the opening from front to back.
■ If the drawer front is to fit within the cabinet, deduct its thickness.
■ Deduct twice the thickness of a corner joint (A).

Three sided drawer sides

■ Measure the opening from front to back.
■ If the drawer front is to fit within the cabinet, deduct its thickness.
■ Deduct the thickness of a corner joint (A).
■ Deduct the thickness of a front fixing plate (C).

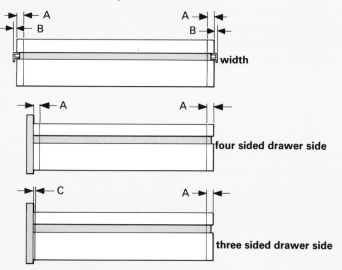

width

four sided drawer side

three sided drawer side

Make these deductions from the size of the cabinet to arrive at the final dimensions. Overall length of the sides will be shorter by the thickness of the drawer front if you want this to fit back into the cabinet instead of overhanging the front.

FITTING OUT A WARDROBE

Modern fittings make it easy to put together a wardrobe interior that suits your storage needs perfectly – whether you use a ready-made kit or separate units.

If you already have a built-in cupboard or sliding door wardrobe, now could be the perfect time to think about organizing the space more efficiently. And if you are installing wardrobe doors, you can plan and fit out the interior at the same time.

Narrowing the choice

The first step is to think about what's going in the wardrobe, and how you'd like to store it. Broadly, there is a choice between hanging space, open storage, and drawers – with special fittings for things like shoes and ties.

The three basic kit options are shown below, and in larger wardrobes there's no reason why you shouldn't combine them. But before you decide, run through *Planning your storage needs* overleaf.

A typical wardrobe interior kit
(right) providing a practical mix of different storage including dividers, hanging rails, drawers and open shelving.

....Shopping List....

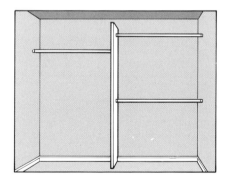

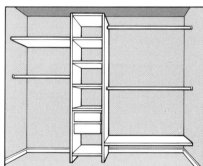

Rail/divider system

The simplest type of interior kit, consisting of one or more vertical panels to divide the wardrobe, plus hanging rails and hooks. Shelves are a make-yourself option.
You need a minimum of 300mm (12″) depth for the unit, but at least 600mm (2′) if you want to hang clothes. A single kit spans up to about 2.4m (8′).
You may need 300×15mm (12×⅝″) melamine-faced boards for shelves.

Shelf/drawer system

This type of self-assembly kit has vertical box frames which include shelves and drawers. Hanging rails fit onto each side and you can make your own top and bottom shelves.
You need at least 400mm (16″) depth for the unit, rising to 600mm (2′) for hanging clothes. A kit typically spans up to about 2.4m (8′); above this, buy two kits.
You may need 450×15mm (18×⅝″) melamine-faced boards for shelves.

Wire basket system

This is based on open frames made of plastic-coated wire which clip together to make rigid supports. There is a wide range of baskets, hooks and rails for varied storage.
You need 300-550mm (12-22″) depth, depending on the system, and at least 600mm (2′) if you want to hang clothes.
You may need 15mm melamine-faced boards for shelving, and hanging rails may be separate.

PLANNING YOUR STORAGE NEEDS

Different things need different kinds of storage, but a combination of these four basic types will cope with most needs:

Hanging space: Rails for hanging clothes are a top priority. Long dresses and coats need more height than jackets, trousers, suits, skirts and shirts.

Open shelving and drawers: Shelving is useful for items like bed linen, towels and luggage if this is stored in the bedroom. Drawers are best for small objects, underwear and folded knitwear.

Special storage may be required for things like ties and shoes.

Only you can decide how much of each type you need – people are different sizes, and so are their clothes. To give yourself a clearer idea, draw up a detailed list of what you want to store and divide the items between the four categories listed above. Then allocate space accordingly.

HANGING SPACE

The main hanging rails should be set slightly above eye level, around 1.8m (6′) from the floor – and if there is a top shelf, you need at least 50mm clearance above the rails to unhook a hanger. Clothes are deceptively heavy, so avoid very long, unsupported spans.

Remember that where clothes don't need the full hanging height, you can fit shelves or a second rail below them to make better use of the space.

These are the approximate hanging lengths needed for different types of clothing:
- Long dress: 1.6m (5′4″).
- Dressing gown, robe or long

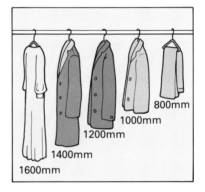

Unless you have lots of full-length clothes you can fit other storage in the unused space below the hanging rail – a second rail, perhaps, or a low shelf unit.

A drawer/shelf system cuts down on clutter by providing easily accessible storage for small or awkward items, as well as folded clothes and towels.

DRAWERS AND OPEN SHELVING

You could easily need anywhere from 10 to 15 drawers for folded clothes, depending on their size and the number you want to store. But some clothes can be kept in open shelves or wire baskets just as well, saving on drawer space.

Spare bedlinen and luggage is likely to need anywhere between about 1m (3′4″) and 3m (10′) total shelf length. But suitcases may be very wasteful of space unless they can be fitted inside one another.

Shoes, handbags, hats and so on will probably require 1-2m (3-7′) total shelving space, with plenty of room above for taller items. But you may be able to store them more efficiently by using purpose-made racks or hooks.

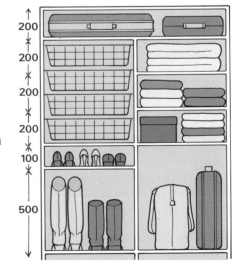

Most people need a mix of shelf and drawer spacing to cope with all that they want to store. Some tall items can be highly wasteful of wardrobe space.

coat: 1.4m (4'6").
■ Medium coat, man's jacket: 1.2m (4').
■ Woman's jacket, skirt: 1m (3'4").
■ Trousers, shirts: 800mm (32").

A lot obviously depends on how much you have to store, but as a rule of thumb most men need a total hanging space about 650mm (26") wide, while women need around 1m (3'4").

If you have a lot of clothes needing hangers, this could go up to about 1.5m (5') for men and 2.4m (8') for women. And if you hang shirts and blouses, add about another 300-500mm (12-20") to the basic measurements.

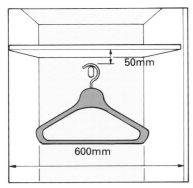

Plenty of clearance *is needed for the hanging rails. You need room to lift clothes on and off, and enough depth for them to hang without crushing.*

This rail/divider system *lets you hang short clothes on two levels to make the best use of space. You can add shelves to take other items which can't be hung on rails.*

Wire baskets *are a good alternative storage solution for the kind of things which need to go in drawers or on shelves – and they ensure that everything gets properly aired.*

49

FITTING A RAIL/DIVIDER

The maximum span of a wardrobe rail before it starts to bend or sag is usually about 1200mm (4'). This is narrower than most wardrobes, so the simplest type of rail system consists of upright panels which divide the wardrobe into short sections with hanger rails fitted on either side. All these parts come as a kit, which also includes hooks and other fittings.

For a short two-door wardrobe, you need only one centre panel. This is normally supplied with three rails to span the space from it to the sides of the wardrobe. For wider wardrobes, simply buy an extra kit to make up the kind of layout shown below. Top and bottom shelves aren't included; make these from standard shelf-width boards.

Tools: electric drill and bits, spirit level, tape measure, junior hacksaw, handsaw and screwdrivers.

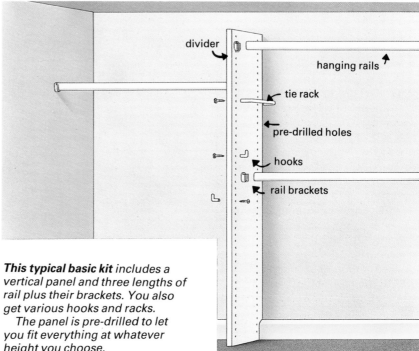

This typical basic kit includes a vertical panel and three lengths of rail plus their brackets. You also get various hooks and racks.

The panel is pre-drilled to let you fit everything at whatever height you choose.

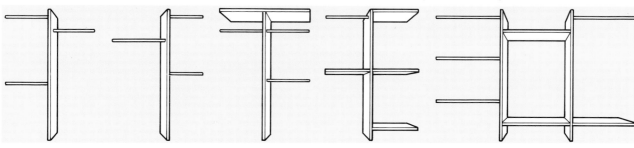

Fit the rails at any height you like on either side of the panel.

Optional shelves can be added by using standard boards.

In a wide wardrobe, combine two kits side-by-side.

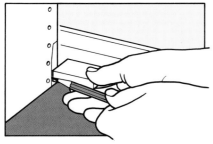

1 Scribe the vertical panel to clear a skirting by standing it the same distance out from the wall as the width of the scribing block. Saw out the notch.

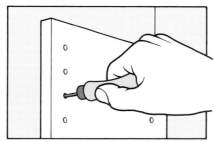

2 Stand the panel against the end of the wardrobe or the side wall and mark off the heights of the rails on both the panel and the side.

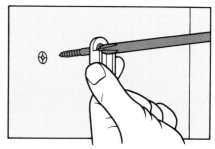

3 Screw the hanging rail brackets to the panel and to the end of the wardrobe or side wall. Use wallplugs if you're fixing into masonry.

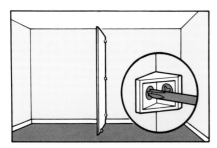

4 Fix the vertical panel in place using plastic joint blocks or brackets screwed into drilled and plugged holes in the wall behind. Screw another block to the floor.

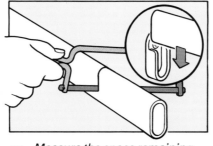

5 Measure the space remaining for each rail between the panel and the end, and cut them to length with a junior hacksaw. Fit the rails to the brackets.

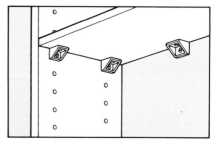

6 If you want to add shelves, cut them from melamine-faced board and attach them to the sides, back and vertical panel using joint blocks.

FITTING A SHELF/DRAWER UNIT

This works in a similar way to the simple rail/divider system on the previous page. It has a number of hanging rails, plus a vertical divider to break up the interior of the wardrobe into short, easily spanned lengths. But in this case the vertical divider is a free-standing box unit containing shelves and drawers. The system comes in flat-packed form, so you can fix the shelves at the height of your choice.

Like the simpler rail/divider system, you can fit a single kit to a narrow wardrobe, or combine two to cope with a wider span (see below). It's also possible to add extra top or bottom shelves to the kit, using lengths of standard shelf-width sized melamine-faced board.

Tools: electric drill and bits, spirit level, tape measure, junior hacksaw, handsaw and screwdrivers.

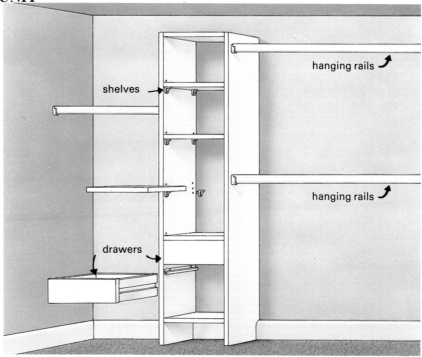

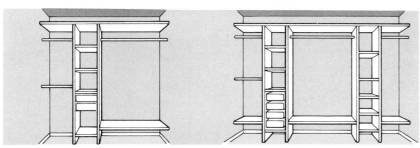

The kit includes (above) *a flat-pack storage unit consisting of two sides, connecting shelves and a set of drawers. There are also lengths of rail and brackets to fit on each side of the assembled unit. The rails are often different lengths, allowing you to stand the divider off to one side of the wardrobe.*

Fit the rails *at any height you want and add your own shelves.*

Two kits *allow for more varied storage in a wider wardrobe.*

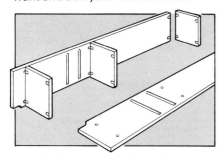

1 Scribe the vertical panels to fit over any skirting. Then fix drawer runners and shelves to assemble the unit – normally using screws and plastic blocks.

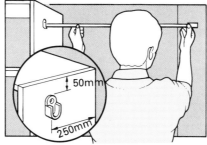

2 Stand the unit up and mark the height of the hanging rail bracket on the vertical panel. Measure to the wall or end of the wardrobe to find the rail length.

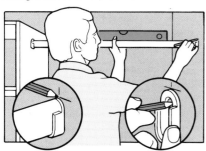

3 Screw the bracket to the vertical panel. Cut the rail to length with a junior hacksaw, then find the position of the other bracket and screw in place.

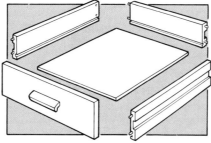

4 Assemble the drawers, which are supplied in flat-pack form with either plastic joints or glued corners. Fit these and the internal shelves in place.

Trade tip

Forward planning

❝ Don't make the mistake I once did and forget the space left when the wardrobe doors are opened. The interior unit must be offset to one side so that it is completely unobstructed by the doors – otherwise you won't be able to pull out the drawers.

Think about this at the planning stage, because it may affect the way you arrange your hanging space. ❞

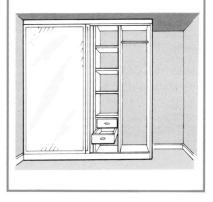

WIRE BASKET SYSTEMS

Wire basket storage units can be free-standing, or supported by the side panels of the wardrobe. Kits range from complete wardrobe interiors to individual baskets and small modules which can be fitted into any odd space. Some allow you to use the baskets as ordinary drawers, and you can also get accessories like undershelf baskets and shoe racks.

A typical basic system consists of a set of side panels, crossbars and baskets, made in a range of sizes so that you can assemble sets of units to suit your needs. Most systems are based on a standard unit width (often 450mm – 18″), so you can combine them to span any area.

Wire basket components vary but this typical system shows many of the fittings available. Open baskets are used as drawers, and shelves or hanging rails clip on.

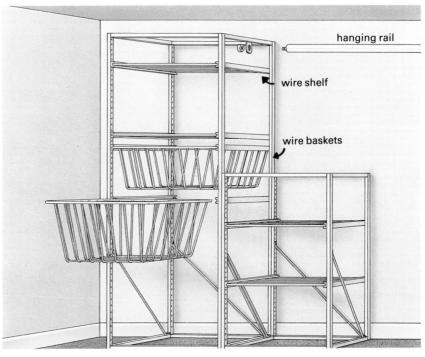

hanging rail

wire shelf

wire baskets

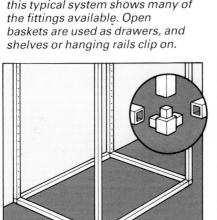

1 *Free-standing frames clip together using crossbars at top and bottom. Press them together by hand or use a mallet if they are stiff.*

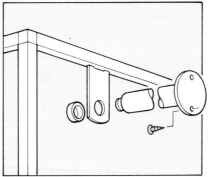

2 *Some systems have attachments for hanging rails. The other end of the rail can be supported by a bracket screwed to the end panel or side wall.*

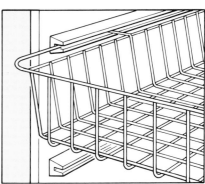

3 *Many wire baskets can also be used as open drawers in a unit made from solid boards. This is done by fitting separate runners to the insides of the panels.*

PROBLEM SOLVER

Dealing with awkward corners

Shallow wardrobes and ones where the depth is reduced by a projection inside, such as an old chimney breast, pose special problems – because you need about 600mm (2′) to fit in a hanger comfortably.

If you haven't enough depth, one answer may be to hang the clothes facing the front of the wardrobe instead of sideways on. You'll be able to get at them easily by fitting an extending wardrobe rail running from front to back. These are especially good for hanging light clothes like shirts and blouses.

You need a space at least 600mm wide, and a sturdy shelf above it, into which to screw the new extending rail.

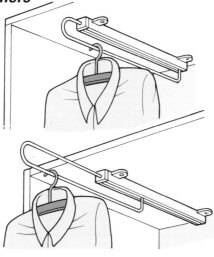

This type of rail needs less than 400mm fitting depth but can be pulled out for easy access.

Trade tip

Heavy loads

❝ If you've got a lot of jackets and coats to store, they can be surprisingly heavy. Oval hanging rails are much better than round ones at taking the strain and are used in most kits. You can also buy them separately.

Whatever type of rail you are fixing, bear in mind that the heavy weights involved mean that you need good fastenings.

I recommend using chipboard screws in all types of wood, as these are much better at getting a grip. For very long rails or very heavy loads, consider fitting a top shelf and screwing a centre support bracket underneath.❞

FITTING SLIDING WARDROBE DOORS

....Shopping List....

Track kits contain double top and bottom tracks, a clip-on fascia panel, and fixings. They come in standard widths which you trim to size.

'DIY door' kits come with tracks, runners and clip-on frames for the doors.

For the doors themselves, use 4mm plywood. This is generally available in 2440×1220mm (8×4') sheets, in two grades.

Sliding door kits for mirror and panel doors are sold in one, two, three and four-door packs. The doors come in one height, but a range of widths.

Tools checklist: Tape measure, drill, junior hacksaw, various screwdrivers. You will need other tools and materials for making your own doors or adapting the opening size, so run through the instructions before you start. Before you decide finally what kits to buy, work out how and where you're going to fit the wardrobe (see overleaf).

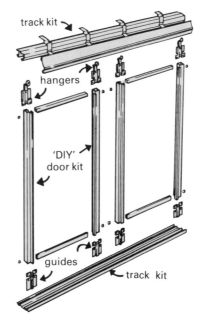

track kit

hangers

'DIY' door kit

guides

track kit

Installing a set of sliding wardrobe doors is a simple yet effective way to streamline your bedroom storage. The doors enclose as much space as you want and can also be used to conceal untidy features in the room. There's a choice of styles, including mirror and panel fronts.

Two systems are available. One consists of two separate kits – a door pack, which includes standard size doors and runners; and a track pack containing the top and bottom tracks, plus a clip-on fascia.

The other system is based around a 'DIY door' kit containing the tracks, together with clip-on frames for the doors. You provide the actual door panels, which has the advantage that you can cut them to size and paint or paper them to match the room.

Both types are extremely versatile – run the doors right across the room; stop them short with an end panel, or fit them in an alcove.

Once you have enclosed the space, fit out the inside to suit your requirements. Special wardrobe interior kits – covered later in Home Improver – make this a quick and simple job. Alternatively, fit a plain hanging rail.

THE RIGHT COMBINATION

The secret of a trouble-free installation is to balance the look you want against a layout which suits the room and is easy to arrange. So before you order any parts, consider these points:

Which doors? Mirror and panel door kits normally come in a standard height of 2285mm (90″), which rounds off to fit a ceiling height of 2.5m (8′2″) by the time they're fitted in their tracks. They can't be cut down, which rules out using them if your ceiling is lower than their standard height. But if the ceiling is higher than this, it's relatively easy to make up the difference with a timber filling piece or even a false 'drop top' panel (see Problem Solver, page 58).

With 'DIY' doors, you can cut the plywood panels to any size you like so long as the floor and ceiling are reasonably level. You may prefer this option anyway if you're on a tight budget, or you want to decorate the panels to match the rest of the room.

Which layout? The box below shows the possible variations, depending on how your room is laid out and what other furniture has to go in it. If necessary, draw a sketch plan to make sure the new layout won't be too cramped.

Before making a final decision, read through *Where to fix the top track* opposite. If the ceiling joists are inconveniently placed, it may be easier to alter the depth of the wardrobe than to add bracing.

How many doors? When you've decided on your ideal layout, measure the opening width. Then check the chart at the bottom of the page which shows the width and number of doors needed for a range of given openings.

- If you're fitting 'DIY doors', use the chart to work out what size to make the panels.
- If you choose standard doors, but you're fitting an end panel, arrange for the opening width to match one of the combinations in the chart.
- If you want standard doors to run wall to wall, and the opening width doesn't match any of the standard sizes, you have the choice of shortening the wardrobe with an end panel or fitting side panels to make up the difference.

WHICH LAYOUT?

Run the wardrobe wall to wall (right) using two, three or four doors as appropriate. If the doors are a fixed size, you may have to fit one or more side panels to take up the extra opening width.

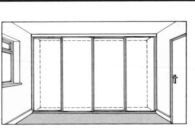

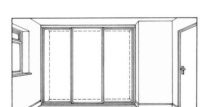

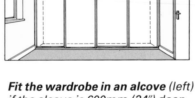

Fit the wardrobe in an alcove (left) if the alcove is 600mm (24″) deep or more. Otherwise, it's more practical to increase the depth with an end panel or continue the doors across the entire wall.

Where space is limited, stop the wardrobe short and fit your own end panel. Alternatively, place the wardrobe in the middle of the wall and fit two end panels. Both options allow you to match the opening width to standard doors.

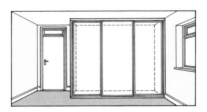

Mirror doors (above) blend easily into any decorative scheme and have the advantage of making a room seem larger. However, they can't be cut, so you may need to fit side panels to make up the opening width.
Panel doors (right) come ready finished and have a pleasingly substantial appearance. Like mirror doors they can't be cut.

WHICH DOOR SIZE?

The chart shows commonly available sizes of mirror and panel doors. If you make your own doors, use one of the combinations shown to work out the width of the plywood panels.

Opening width	Number and size of doors required	Opening width	Number and size of doors required
1190mm (3′11″)	2×609mm (2′)	2235mm (7′4″)	3×750mm (2′6″)
1498mm (4′11″)	2×760mm (2′6″)	2690mm (8′10″)	3×900mm (3′)
1803mm (5′11″)	2×914mm (3′)	2950mm (9′8″)	4×750mm (2′6″)
1778mm (5′10″)	3×609mm (2′)	3600mm (11′10″)	4×900mm (3′)

WHERE TO FIT THE TOP TRACK

Your wardrobe should be around 600mm (24") deep to allow for clothes on hangers, with the top track positioned to suit (in most kits it goes 25mm (1") inside the line of the doors).

However, because this track takes the weight of the doors, it can't be fixed to the thin ceiling plaster – you need to screw it directly into the supporting timbers (joists).

Start by finding out which way the joists run. If the floor upstairs is boarded, the boards will run in the opposite direction, with rows of nails giving away the joists' exact positions.

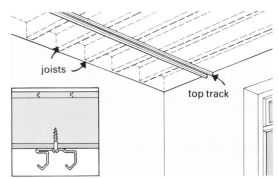

If the joists run at right angles to the track, there are no problems. Simply drill extra fixing holes in the track to match the joist spacing, then screw the track in position.

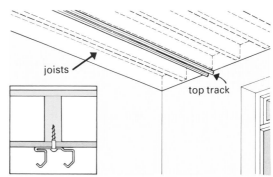

If the joists are parallel to the track, try to arrange for the track to run along the centre of a joist – if necessary by increasing or reducing the depth of the wardrobe slightly.

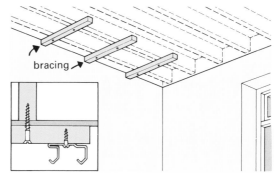

Alternatively, fix the track to 50×50mm (2×2") bracing pieces fitted between the two nearest joists. The neat way is to nail these from above; but if you don't have access, screw them from below then hide the ends with a piece of timber.

FITTING THE TRACKS

Having taken delivery of the kit parts, check the dimensions of the opening as follows:

Width Measure from wall to wall or to the end panel position. If you need to close up the opening to fit the doors, see Problem Solver overleaf for how to do it.

Height Measure from floor to ceiling at several points. If you need to fit filling pieces or a panel to accommodate the doors, again see Problem Solver overleaf.

If you find the door-plus-track height – 2.5m (8'2") for standard doors – varies by more than 12mm (½"), one or other of the tracks will need packing with slips of stiff card or hardboard to bring them level. Insert the packing before tightening the track fixing screws.

Unless you are fitting a filling piece below it, the bottom track can be fixed directly to the floor through the existing covering. Take extra care that it aligns with the top track.

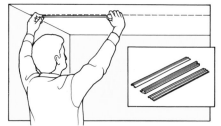

1 Mark the final width of the wardrobe on the tracks and fascia. Square cutting lines across them, then saw them to length using a junior hacksaw.

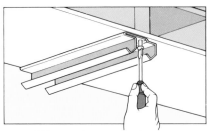

2 Offer up the top track and mark the fixing positions (drill extra holes if necessary). Screw the track in place, leaving the screws slightly loose.

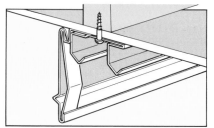

3 Clip the fascia over the top track as shown. When it's in position, tighten the track fixing screws to clamp the fascia against the ceiling.

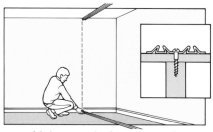

4 Make sure the bottom track aligns exactly with the top one when marking the fixing positions. If necessary, pack underneath to bring it level.

Trade tip

A head for heights

❝ Measuring from the floor to the ceiling accurately can be tricky. I find the easiest way to do it is to take two battens about 1.8m (6') long and tape them or bind them together with elastic bands so that they fit the height exactly.

Then I can measure them to check the height or try them at different points to see if the dimensions vary from one side of the room to the other. ❞

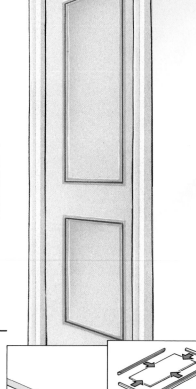

HANGING THE DOORS

If you're fitting standard size doors, the tricky part of the job is out of the way. The hangers and guides are factory fitted, so simply slip the doors into their tracks and adjust the guides following the kit maker's instructions.

If you are making your own doors, now is the time to cut the plywood panels to size.

Measure up with the tracks in place, allowing for the extra taken up by the runners and guides. If you're trimming the width as well as the height, double doors are cut to half the width plus a 25mm (1") overlap allowance, while three-door sets are cut to a third of the opening width, plus the overlap.

Cut the door panels as accurately as you can, but don't worry about finishing the edges: these are hidden by the frames, which you measure direct from the panels and cut separately. Check each panel's fit before cutting the frames.

1 Having transferred the measurements of the opening to the panels, cut them to size using a handsaw or electric jigsaw fitted with a fine blade.

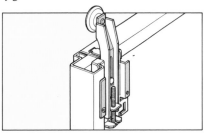

3 The top hangers and bottom guides have tabs which normally clip into slots in the frame. If these were sawn off, fit them with screws instead.

2 Use a junior hacksaw to cut the frame pieces, sizing them directly from the cut panels. Notch the corners where they join, then clip them in place.

4 Hook the hanger wheels on the tracks by offering up the doors at an angle. When in place, align by adjusting the hangers; lastly, fit the runners.

56

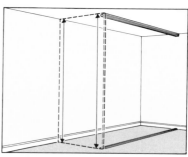

fascia clipped to top track

top track fixed to ceiling joist(s)

bottom track fixed to floor

A typical 3-door assembly (above) using standard size mirror and panel doors. When combining door types, fit the mirror on the front of the two track channels.
Angle the doors (right) when slotting in the hangers.

ADDING AN END PANEL

Where the wardrobe isn't running from wall to wall, fit an end panel of 16mm or 19mm board (such as veneered chipboard). Buy a piece long enough to fit from floor to ceiling and wide enough to fit from the back wall to the front of the fascia.

Almost certainly, you'll need to trim the panel to fit against the wall and ceiling, so cut it on the generous side to begin with, then scribe and fine-trim it afterwards.

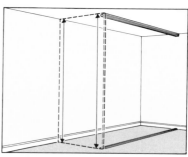

1 Measure the height from floor to ceiling at the front and back of the wardrobe. Mark the dimensions on the panel and cut it to size.

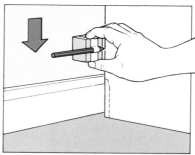

2 Stand the panel up and scribe the back edge to fit the wall and skirting. Then trim it with a hand saw or jigsaw, and finish the edge with a surform plane.

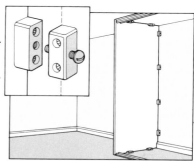

3 Fix the panel with plastic joint blocks. Fit the two top and bottom; along the back edge, space four evenly and screw them into drilled and plugged holes.

Adjusting the opening height

How you approach this depends on the size of the gap.

■ For gaps up to 100mm (4"), fit a timber filling piece under the bottom track using either of the methods shown on the right.

The thickness of the timber doesn't have to match the gap exactly – remember, the runners will accommodate differences up to 12mm (½"). If the floor level is out by more than this, pack under the filling piece with slips of wood or hardboard.

■ For gaps between 100mm and 200mm (4-8"), you can fit a filling piece top *and* bottom – but only if the floor and ceiling are roughly level. Otherwise, see below.

■ For larger gaps, build a 'drop top' frame of 100×50mm (4×2") timber as shown on the right, then screw the top track to this.

Give the frame members as much support as possible, screwing them to the joists where appropriate, and to a bearer fixed along the back wall.

Afterwards, panel the frame with 6mm plywood pinned to the frame and then decorate to match the walls.

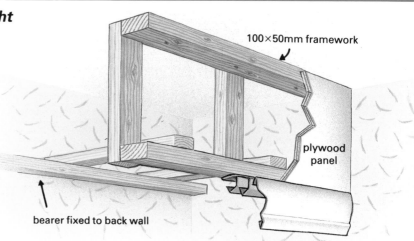

100×50mm framework

plywood panel

bearer fixed to back wall

Make a 'drop top' frame from 100×50mm (4×2") timber screwed to the ceiling with braces extending to the back wall.

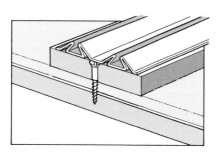

For gaps of up to 100mm (4"), it's easiest to screw a filler piece under the bottom track. Choose a thickness that comes within 12mm (½") of the gap.

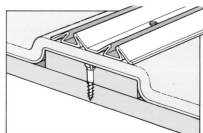

Alternatively, for a small gap roll back the carpet and fit the filling piece underneath. (This is also better if you need to level the timber with packing pieces.)

Adjusting the opening width

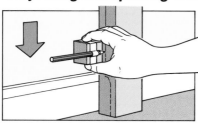

1 *If the filling piece has to clear a skirting, stand it in place temporarily and scribe the skirting's shape as shown using a pencil and block of wood.*

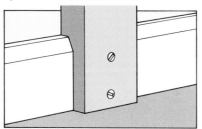

2 *Cut out the notch with a hand saw then screw the filling piece to the wall. Check that it sits vertically – if not, pack behind it.*

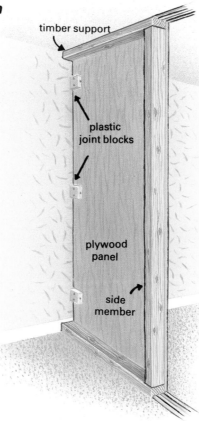

timber support

plastic joint blocks

plywood panel

side member

Like the height, how you deal with the opening width depends on the gap.

■ For gaps up to 100mm (4"), fit a filling piece to the adjoining wall. Screw it just behind the line of the fascia, and pack behind it to ensure that it's vertical. Fill any gaps later.

Use the same technique to clear a projecting skirting board. Shape the end of the filling piece to fit the skirting as shown on the left.

■ For gaps of between 100mm and 200mm (4-8"), fit a filling piece on both sides.

■ For larger gaps, fit a filling panel as shown on the left.

If the panel is running to ceiling height, fix the 100×50mm (4×2") side member to timber supports screwed to the ceiling and floor. If you're building a drop top panel as well, incorporate the side member into the rest of the frame. Fix the panel itself with plastic joint blocks.

MODULAR BEDROOM FURNITURE

Self-assembly modular systems give any bedroom the looks and style of hand-made, built-in furniture. They are easy to build and, unlike made-to-measure fitments, they can be adapted to meet any storage needs. This flexibility comes from using standard units which can fit together in many different ways.

Modular bedroom furniture is sold by superstores as well as furniture shops and specialist suppliers. There are two basic types:

Type A systems look like conventional 'bedroom suite' furniture, but unlike separate units they are designed to join together to suit the room setting. Cupboard units can also be linked with a continuous work surface. There is a variety of different styles, with options for internal fittings and trims.

Type B systems are based on 'boxes' in a small range of standard sizes which screw together or stack to make wardrobes, cupboards, dressing tables and chests of drawers. There is a choice of front panels, doors, tops and trims to adapt the boxes to different styles.

Self-assembly modular furniture (below) is an ideal way to design a fully-fitted, stylish bedroom.

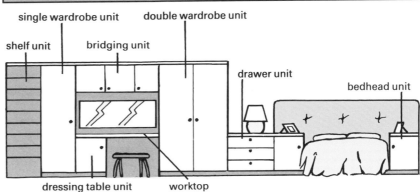

.... Shopping List ....

single wardrobe unit • double wardrobe unit • shelf unit • bridging unit • drawer unit • bedhead unit • dressing table unit • worktop

The number and type of units varies between makes, but a typical system (Type A or B) might offer:

Single wardrobe units with rails and shelves or drawers.

Double wardrobe units twice as wide as the single wardrobes.

Drawer units shorter and shallower than wardrobes, but the same widths.

Bridging units in modular widths for high level storage.

Dressing table units – often a top fitted over two drawer units.

Bedhead units/headboards.

Open shelves in modular dimensions, but often shallower.

Worktops to fit individual drawer units or span a run of units.

Corner units (a few systems only).

Trims including *fascias, plinths* and *cornices* in various styles. Doors, drawer fronts and handles may also be supplied separately.

Accessories include *mirrors, concealed lighting, adjustable shelving* and *hanging rails*.

Tools checklist: Only basic tools are needed to assemble the units and fix them to the walls. These include a range of screwdrivers, bradawl, tape measure and marking tools, panel saw, tenon saw, electric drill and hammer.

PLANNING A SYSTEM

Although some suppliers offer a design service, doing it yourself gives you a clearer idea of the options, whichever range you finally choose. This is what's involved:

Make a checklist of the units you want, based on modules available.

■ Work out how much rail you need for hanging clothes, plus 10% for future purchases. Each single wardrobe has about half a metre of rail, so to make up 2m (6'6"), say, you could use one double wardrobe and two singles (for short clothes like shirts, an alternative is to use a single and fit a double tier of rails).

■ Work out which units give the number of drawers/shelves you need.

■ Add a dressing table and any 'special purpose' units to the list.

Draw a scale plan of the room, showing windows, doors, power points and fixed obstacles. Work on squared paper, based on the modular size.

■ Ink in the position of the bed, or cut it out of paper to scale if you want to try moving it around.

■ Pencil three lines round the plan. Draw the first at the depth of a drawer unit. Draw the second at the depth of a wardrobe unit. Draw the third about 500mm (20") beyond this to show opening space of door.

Try the units in position by drawing them in pencil or positioning paper cut-outs on the plan.

■ Wardrobes need a clear wall, but drawer units can go below a window. If power points are in the way, have them moved.

■ Allow about 700mm (28") space for making the bed.

■ To fit units into corners, see the alternatives given below. Any odd gaps can be concealed later.

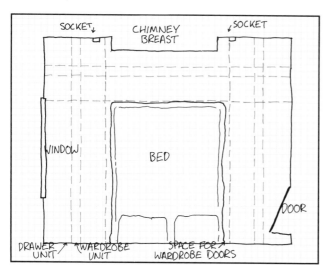

Draw a plan showing the bed and fixed points. Draw lines around the edge to show the various unit depths.

Pencil in the units on your checklist. Try different layouts to find the best arrangement within the space.

Trade tip

Door openings

❝ When you draw your plans, bear in mind that the doors on single units can normally be hung to open either way round. Make sure your plan indicates which is the best opening direction, taking into account the position of other furniture in the room. ❞

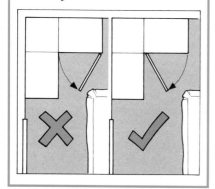

Dressing tables can be built up with a special unit supported on two drawer units (as right) or between a pair of wardrobes. Site them where there is plenty of light and a power point nearby.

STANDARD MODULE SIZES

Check the detailed dimensions given for each module before drawing them on your plan. The measurements given here are representative of popular ranges, but will vary slightly from one make to another.

Module dimensions also differ according to the type of system:
Type A units are normally based around a range of different dimensions. However, there are several standard depths, and the widths of double units are always exactly twice those of the singles.
Type B units generally come in fewer sizes, with much more standardized dimensions. All take drawers or shelves, and all but the smallest take hanging rails, so each unit can be fitted out for different purposes – giving plenty of flexibility.

A typical system comes in three heights which are available in two widths; all are based on multiples of metres or half metres. Full height units are deeper than the half and quarter height units.

TYPE 'A' UNIT DIMENSIONS

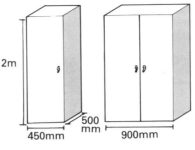

wardrobe units

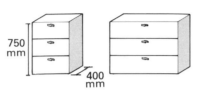

drawer units

bridging units

TYPE 'B' UNIT DIMENSIONS

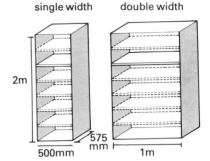

full height (for wardrobes)

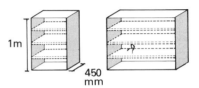

half height (for chests)

quarter height (for chests and bridging units)

Corner units are available in many ranges. Wardrobe space can only be reached through the open door to one side of the corner (above). With low units, however, you can fit a lift-up lid in the worktop (right) to conceal a linen basket tucked neatly away in the angle.

TURNING CORNERS

There are two ways of fitting bedroom units round a corner, so check what's available for your chosen system:

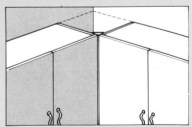

Leaving the corner empty and fitting a corner post is only worth doing if you fit more than a single unit on the side wall.

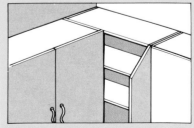

Fitting a double unit in the corner and butting a second unit against it can leave the storage space awkward to reach.

ASSEMBLING THE UNITS

Bedroom furniture comes flat-packed for home assembly, and is put together in the following way. First, assemble the basic carcases. All the units consist of two sides, a top, bottom and back panel, and the corners are jointed with screws or knock-down fittings. There may be additional fixed shelves or bracing bars, especially on tall units. Other fittings are added later.

Drawers, shelves and doors are added to the basic carcases once they have been assembled. It's best to leave this until the units are fitted in place, so that they will be light and easy to handle.

Side panels are pre-drilled for shelves, drawer runners and hinges. It is often easier to add these fittings before assembly.

cross bar

joining strip

top

Back panels are sometimes in two halves with a joining strip. They normally slide into grooves and are pinned.

chipboard screw

Structural shelves and cross bars fix to the side panels to brace the structure.

base

side panel

joint fitting

On many systems the base has adjustable feet which will be concealed behind a plinth at a later stage.

Fix the corners of the carcase using the screws or knock-down fittings supplied.

BUILDING UP THE SYSTEM

Referring to your plan, build up the units in the room in this order:
- Stand a wardrobe unit in place to set the levels.
- Try the other units in position, especially if they are a tight fit.
- If everything is OK, fix the first wardrobe in place.
- Fit any modules – eg bridging units – which go next to the first wardrobe. If necessary, use a second wardrobe to ensure that everything lines up as it should.
- Build outwards in this way, joining the units together for support.

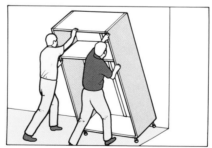

1 *Stand wardrobe units carefully so you don't strain the corner feet, and take care not to bump the top on the ceiling. Manoeuvre the unit into the right position.*

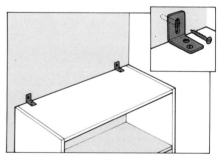

2 *Use the adjuster feet or packing pieces to ensure the wardrobe is level. For security when finally positioned, fix the top to the wall with brackets.*

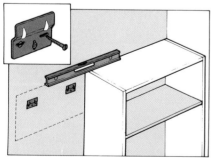

3 *Bridging units are hung on wall brackets, which may be adjustable. Mark the level from the wardrobes on either side, then drill and plug the fixings.*

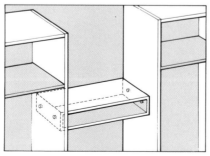

4 *In some systems, dressing table units are bolted through the sides of the two adjoining modules. Take care that they align properly on both sides.*

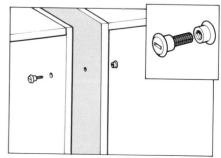

5 *Join all units with connector bolts through drilled holes in the sides. Use the same method to fix any units which you are stacking on top of one another.*

FITTING SHELVES AND HANGING RAILS

Shelves may be structural – in which case they are rigidly fixed to hold the carcase together (see left). But many shelves are adjustable, and are normally supported on studs.

Hanging rails are held on with brackets screwed to the inside of the carcase. Oval section rails (which are stronger than round ones) are most common, and the brackets normally have a double fixing. This consists of a push-in peg on the back which fits whichever pre-drilled hole is at the right height, plus a screw to keep the bracket in place.

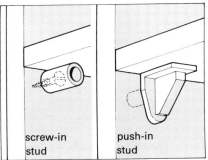

screw-in stud   push-in stud

Adjustable shelves are designed to sit loose on supporting studs which either screw to the sides of the carcase or push into pre-drilled holes.

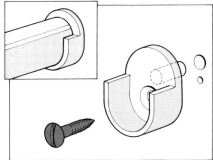

To fit hanging rails, position the brackets on the end panels using the pre-drilled holes. Secure with screws and drop the rail into place.

DOORS, DRAWERS AND WORKTOPS

Fit these after the units have been assembled, aligned and connected.

Doors are designed to be lined up after fitting using levelling screws fitted to the hinges.

Drawers may be made from clip-together plastic mouldings or jointed sections of board. Once assembled, the drawers simply slide on to the runners in the frame. But in some cases the fronts are separate panels which you fit and align after the drawers are in place.

Worktops come either as separate panels to fit individual units, or as continuous lengths which you cut to fit a run of cupboards. Corner joints in the worktop can be made by using special fillets.

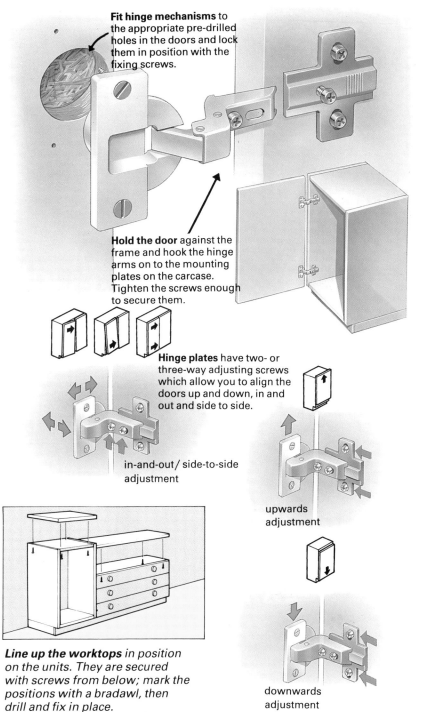

Fit hinge mechanisms to the appropriate pre-drilled holes in the doors and lock them in position with the fixing screws.

Hold the door against the frame and hook the hinge arms on to the mounting plates on the carcase. Tighten the screws enough to secure them.

Hinge plates have two- or three-way adjusting screws which allow you to align the doors up and down, in and out and side to side.

in-and-out/side-to-side adjustment

upwards adjustment

downwards adjustment

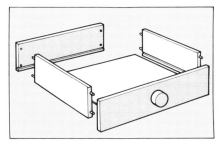

Drawers normally consist of four jointed sections which you assemble around a baseboard. Squeeze household glue into the joints for extra strength.

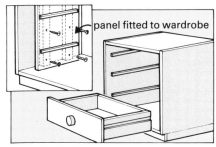

panel fitted to wardrobe

Slide the drawers on to their runners, which are fitted inside the carcase. Wardrobes may need to be fitted with extra panels to support the runners.

Line up the worktops in position on the units. They are secured with screws from below; mark the positions with a bradawl, then drill and fix in place.

FINISHING TOUCHES

With the units assembled and the main fittings in place, the final stage is to add the trim pieces and handles.

Various trims are supplied to match the style of the doors and drawer fronts. And since they help to give the furniture its 'all-in-one' look, it's worth taking the trouble to fit them neatly.

Cornices are used to finish the tops of the units, and to disguise small gaps between full height units and the ceiling. They are normally supplied in continuous lengths which you cut to fit and then screw to the unit panels. See Problem Solver below for how to mitre the corners to a neat finish.

Plinth panels simply need cutting squarely to length with a panel saw or tenon saw. They are usually fitted with concealed clip fixings.

Handles are easy to fit. The holes in the units are often part-drilled, allowing you a choice of positions.

Other trims include mouldings to fit below a bridging unit. These are usually glued or pinned in place. Door and drawer trims are fitted in the same way.

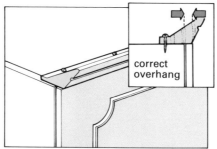

Cornices are secured by screwing them down to the tops of the units. Make sure they project by the right amount before you mark the holes.

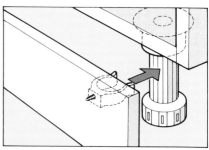

Plinth panels normally have plastic clips to secure them to the adjuster feet. On some systems they screw to the sides of the unit.

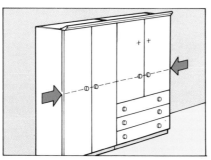

Fit door handles so they align on all the units. Some doors may have alternative positions depending on which way up they are fitted.

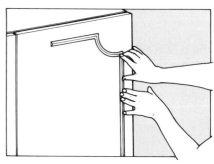

If your units come with stick-on door and drawer trims, fit these last of all to ensure that they line up as accurately as possible.

PROBLEM SOLVER

Concealing gaps

Small gaps are inevitable where units go flush against walls and the walls themselves are out of square. Disguise them with lengths of softwood moulding – *scotia* moulding is a good choice – which are available in various widths up to around 50mm (2"). Afterwards, paint the wood to match either the furniture or the walls.

In most cases you can simply pin the moulding to the units – or even glue it if it is very light. On wider gaps, however, it's better to attach the moulding to a support batten which you can fix to the unit side panel by screwing from inside the carcase.

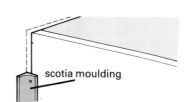

Conceal gaps with softwood moulding (above); you may need a batten support (right).

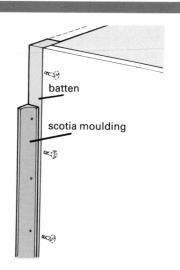

Mitring cornices

Cutting the ends of cornice pieces so that they join in neat, 45° mitres is the one part of the job that demands a fair degree of skill. Do the cutting using a tenon saw and a wooden *mitre box* – an inexpensive tool which has many other uses. It's easier if the box is large enough for the cornice to sit comfortably inside it, though some shapes will need supporting on an offcut (or failing this, a piece of cloth) to steady them.

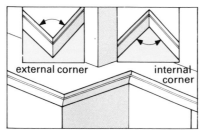

Mark the cornice carefully, noting whether the corner is internal or external. Pencil a rough cutting line to indicate the direction of the mitre.

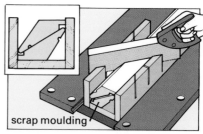

Place the marked length in the mitre box, underside uppermost and supported on an offcut. Align the mark with the appropriate slots and saw gently.

FITTED KITCHENS – BUYING UNITS

For most do-it-yourselfers, buying, planning and installing a new fitted kitchen is one of the most exciting and challenging jobs they're ever likely to undertake. But with so much money involved, it's a subject that demands careful consideration – particularly when deciding what sort of system to go for.

Not surprisingly, most people consider a fitted kitchen an essential part of modern living. The vast majority of kitchens consist of a series of standard-sized modular units which make the best possible use of the available space (a precious commodity in most households), while tough, wipe-clean materials take much of the drudgery out of day-to-day housework.

A fitted kitchen is also an investment – adding substantially to the value of a home. So whether you're starting from scratch, or replacing old units that have seen better days, it makes sense to plan the new kitchen with care.

The current scene

Fitted kitchens have come a long way over the years, and thanks to refinements in manufacturing techniques, modern designs tend to be better made as well as better looking. But selling fitted kitchens is a highly competitive business, and manufacturers are constantly devising new ways to attract customers. This in turn has had a major effect on the way kitchens are planned.

Once, you started with an ideal plan, found the units to suit, then employed someone to install them or fitted them yourself. Now, many suppliers are happy to take care of the layout design and installation for you – providing of course, you choose their products. As a result, deciding what units to buy – and in what form to buy them – has become the first and most important step in kitchen planning.

The following pages reflect the new approach. Pages 65-68 cover the basic buying options: build from scratch, assemble and install flat-packed or ready made units, have the units installed, or order a custom-built system. Pages 69-72 study layout planning in detail, and pages 73-78 present the many extras – from corner carousels to pull-out tables – which are available.

Read through all these pages before making a final decision – after all, you don't want to commit yourself to a particular brand of unit without considering first how they will fit in or what materials they're made of. And even if you eventually decide to leave design and installation to the supplier, it helps to know how the process works so that you can be sure of getting what you really want.

KITCHEN PLANNING STEP-BY-STEP

■ Consider your options – build from scratch, fit flat-packed or ready made units, have units installed, or choose a custom-designed and fitted kitchen.
Ask yourself:
How much of the work do we want to do ourselves?
Do we have the time?
Can we bear the disruption of doing it ourselves?
■ Consider (and preferably draw up) your ideal kitchen layout.
Ask yourself:
Is the basic shape of the kitchen satisfactory?
If not, what major structural modifications are possible?
■ Get an idea of the finish and 'look' you want for the units.
■ Inspect units across the full range of options, and compare prices and finishes.
Ask yourself:
Can we afford the units we like?
Do they come in suitable sizes for the layout we have in mind?
Can we/do we want to re-use existing appliances?
What sort of design/installation service does the supplier offer – and do we really want it?
Could we get nearer our ideal by spending more on the units and doing more of the installation work ourselves?
OR
Could we save money on our ideal kitchen by fitting it ourselves?
OR
Is it worth paying extra for a 'full service' installation?
■ Take dimensions of chosen units and draw up detailed plan.
■ Plan appliance positions and lighting.
■ Note and plan modifications to structure/existing services.
■ Decide on materials for units, worktops, sink, floor, walls.
■ Select appliances, fixtures and fittings.
OR
■ Discuss the above with your supplier's design consultant and then finalize the detailed layout plan.

The fitted kitchen – good looking, convenient and easy to care for, but how do you choose?

FITTED KITCHENS – THE OPTIONS

BUILD YOURSELF

Building kitchen units to match those available commercially isn't as difficult as it first appears. Most units are basically the same under the skin and many of the component parts are available separately from specialist suppliers. If you don't want to make the doors, DIY superstores stock a wide range of ready-made ones.

Advantages
■ The satisfaction of doing everything yourself.
■ Total control over the quality of the workmanship, choice of materials, etc.
■ Complete flexibility over the size and shape of cupboards.

Disadvantages
■ Unlikely to be cheaper than self-assembly units by the time all the costs are added up.
■ Requires considerable all-round DIY skill.
■ Very time-consuming, and for much of the time the existing kitchen will be out of action.
■ No professional advice or design back-up.

SELF-ASSEMBLY

Most of the DIY superstores, and some high street chains supply kitchen units flat-packed for you to assemble and install yourself. You select the units you need – sometimes with the help of a planning service – and take them away or have them delivered. Assembly is definitely a two-person job.

Advantages
■ Probably the most economical way to buy a fitted kitchen.
■ You may be able to take away the units you need immediately: even if they are not in stock, delivery is usually fast.

Disadvantages
■ Self-assembly is likely to take longer than professional installation and for much of the time the existing kitchen will be out of action. In a busy household this needs careful planning.
■ You have the job of disposing of the old kitchen fittings.
■ Assembling the units isn't difficult – but getting them to fit the existing kitchen may be.
■ Units may not come in a wide range of shapes and sizes, which could lead to wasted space in a small or awkwardly shaped room.
■ Choice of materials may be limited and quality can compare unfavourably with more expensive ranges – check before buying.
■ Some suppliers may not offer complementary ranges of appliances and plumbing fittings; this can complicate the planning process.

READY ASSEMBLED UNITS

Some of the superstores sell their units ready assembled. Again, you select the style and plan the kitchen, usually with the help of a planning service.
Units are delivered partly or fully assembled, ready for installation.

Advantages
■ Some ranges are not much more expensive than flat-packed units, and installation is easier.

■ You should get more stable, rigid unit carcases than you would with flat-packed units.

■ Since the carcases are standard sizes, delivery is fast.

Disadvantages
■ You still have the difficult part to do – rerouting services, connecting up, fitting to non-square walls or uneven floors. Some ranges also need fitting out, which can be a fiddly job.

■ The units will take up a lot of extra space while the kitchen is prepared and the old fittings disposed of. Again, this needs careful planning to avoid inconvenience.

INSTALLATION SERVICE

Many of the DIY superstores offer an installation service on either flat-packed or ready assembled units – and if they don't, you could still consider getting a local builder or carpenter to do the work for you. If you are having other work done in the house, it may be more convenient to use the same team of workmen.

Advantages
■ You don't need any special skills – plumbing, electrics, plastering – or equipment. Even with a DIY installation, you're likely to need professionals for some parts of the job.
■ The job should be done more quickly, minimizing disruption.
■ The installers can probably dispose of the old units.

Disadvantages
■ More costly, though, 'all-in' deals can be good value. Much depends on the condition of the existing kitchen.
■ There may be 'hidden' costs if you are using the supplier's installation team: for example, you may have to pay extra for having existing appliances reconnected.

CUSTOM-DESIGNED AND BUILT

Kitchen specialists pride themselves on offering a complete service. You may buy direct from the manufacturer's showrooms, or from an installation company showing a selection of kitchens – usually by a limited range of manufacturers. Some firms also sell direct: you simply arrange for a home visit from a salesman.

In most cases, the company plans the layout around standard-sized units which are built to order. When the units are ready, the old kitchen is gutted and fitted out by a team of installers.

Advantages
■ Plenty of style and material options, though you'll pay a lot more for top quality.

■ Once you've decided what you want and signed on the dotted line, there is little else to worry about: the manufacturers should cope with everything – right down to laying flooring, tiling and decorating if you want.
■ You don't have to 'shop around' for units, appliances, etc.

Disadvantages
■ The cost is bound to be high.
■ Once you commit yourself to a certain range, the choice of finishes and complementary appliances may be quite limited.
■ The process, from conception to final fitting, may take longer than you'd hoped. For example, there will be several weeks' delay while the units are built.

HAND-MADE KITCHENS

Rather than going to a manufacturer who builds units to standard sizes, you can have your kitchen tailor-made. There are a few national firms who will do this, and many small, local outfits. Prices vary widely, according to materials and construction, but may not be as high as you think – especially with local firms.

Advantages
■ May enable you to make better use of your space in a small or irregularly shaped kitchen.
■ Gives you more control – especially over materials – and reflects your individuality.

Disadvanages
■ Still by and large the costliest option.

■ Smaller companies may not offer full design back-up, and are unlikely to have showrooms where you can inspect the quality of the workmanship (in this case, ask to see actual examples of their work).
■ Non-standard units may involve finding non-standard appliances to fit, which can be both costly and time-consuming.
■ Buying appliances, fittings and decorative materials will probably be left to you.

WORTH CONSIDERING

Think about your budget before talking in earnest to kitchen salesmen – you should at least have some idea of your upper price limit. Finance packages offered by kitchen suppliers are easy to arrange and can look very attractive, but you're likely to get a better deal by taking out a loan through a bank or building society – a new kitchen is one of their favourite reasons for lending money.

If your budget is tight but you want some of the refinements of more expensive units, consider enhancing DIY flat-packed or ready assembled 'basic' units with accessories from other sources. For example, specialist suppliers stock waste bins which fit inside cupboards, plastic-coated wire racks to hold spices, pans, etc, and carousel units to make good use of spaces in corners.

Buying secondhand can provide a source of good quality units at bargain prices – check advertisements in the local press. You'll inevitably have to make some compromises – especially if the package includes ready fitted appliances – but the savings could be worth it. You might consider employing a professional to adapt the units if they don't fit exactly. Kitchen showrooms also sell off their display kitchens – and you should be able to buy any extra units you need to match.

Re-using existing appliances may present a problem if you go for an 'all-in' deal, but don't be talked out of it if the appliances in question are perfectly serviceable – look elsewhere for suitable units.

Think about the existing units, appliances and fittings. They may have some secondhand value, which could contribute towards the cost.

DIY installation does at least give you the chance to shop around for the best value. Since all kitchen units are based on modular dimensions, you don't necessarily have to buy everything from the same outlet. For example you can look out for a stouter work surface, and better quality sinks and taps than may be on offer with the units you have chosen.

ASSESSING THE OPTIONS

Although cost is generally the prime consideration when choosing a kitchen, in the early stages of planning it's worth keeping an open mind. Investigate the full range of options and compare prices, so you can see exactly where the money goes.

One of the most important things to decide is whether or not you want to install the kitchen yourself – and if you do, how the potential savings in labour costs measure up against the extra time and disruption involved. Planning the new layout may give you a clearer picture. Replacing old units, for example, is much easier to do yourself than rearranging walls and rerouting services to cope with a major change-around. Choice of materials could also influence your decision; it may be that DIY installation is the only way of affording the units you really want.

Another key question is how long you intend living in the same house. You won't be able to take the kitchen with you, so it probably won't be worth breaking the bank if there's a chance you might move within a year or two.

Other points to consider are listed in the panel on the right.

Pending a final decision, gather together as many brochures and price lists as you can, and take full advantage of what the kitchen salesmen have to offer.

Design services

Suppliers offering a kitchen design and planning service usually make a small charge, refundable if you order one of their kitchens. Although it pays to work out your own layout plan before making a final decision, getting plans drawn up around a particular range which catches your eye can be a useful source of ideas and may help to clarify your thoughts.

Some suppliers give you paper patterns to try out on a floor plan drawn to scale, while others use computers to draw up projections based on your existing kitchen. In either case, you'll need to draw a sketch plan showing the kitchen dimensions in metric. Don't forget to show alcoves, chimney breasts, windows and opening swings of doors.

If you arrange a home visit, the representative will measure up for you. It's unwise to place any kind of firm order at this stage, so to avoid any embarrassment, make it clear from the start what you want.

DECIDING FACTORS
Check the following points when weighing up the pros and cons of various kitchen systems:

■ Are you comparing like with like? What appears to be an economical range of units in the showroom can easily work out more expensive if all you get are the basic carcases. Doors, interior fittings, end panels, worktops and fascias may be optional 'extras'. Sinks, taps, electrical appliances and under-unit lighting are hardly ever included in the basic price.

■ Compare costs between manufacturers by taking a typical unit (say a 500mm wide cupboard with a single drawer) and checking the price in different showrooms.

■ Open and close all the cupboards and drawers and give them the sort of treatment they might get at home: if doors and drawer fronts look crooked and loose in the showroom, where they've only been on display for a short time, the chances are they won't stand up to years of wear and tear.
Often it's the insides of units that betray poor quality. Look for badly fitting joints and unfinished surfaces – sure signs that the manufacturer has cut corners in order to meet the price.

■ Check what accessories are available – and if you want to re-use existing fittings or appliances, ask whether these can be incorporated.

■ Ask about delivery times and possible installation dates where appropriate. You may find some companies can supply the units in a matter of weeks or even days, while with others you have to wait some months.

■ If you are having the kitchen installed professionally, check that estimates cover rerouting and reconnecting services, making good decorations, and disposal of old fittings. Bear in mind that this may involve an extra survey by the installation team.

Some manufacturers offer a kitchen design service, often including a picture, drawn by a computer, of how the new kitchen will look (inset).

FITTED KITCHENS – PLANNING THE LAYOUT

Creating a kitchen that's comfortable and convenient to work in has as much to do with the way it's laid out as it does with the money spent on units and appliances. So even if you're using a supplier's design service, it's worth drawing up an initial plan to find out exactly how your needs can be met.

Experimenting with layouts on a scale plan based around your chosen range of units is a tried and tested way of planning a new kitchen. A supplier will produce a plan anyway, so that you both know what's being ordered. But in many ways it's better to draw up your own first: as well as organizing your thoughts, it can warn of potential problems and help to avoid expensive mistakes. A layout plan also gives you the freedom to change your mind – not an uncommon event for DIY kitchen planners.

First things first

Before you get down to the details, ask yourself whether the basic shell of the kitchen is satisfactory.
■ Is the room large enough? – and if not, can you make more space by knocking down a wall or repositioning a door? These are major jobs, for which you may need a builder, but it's better to spend the money on them now rather than trying to cram in expensive units.
■ Are the floor and walls sound? – again, if there are structural faults or levelling and plastering to be done, now is the time to do them.
■ Are there 'movable' obstructions such as an old floor-mounted boiler, a walk-in larder or unused chimney breast? If they can be re-sited or demolished, you'll have much more flexibility. Demolishing a chimney is another job that is best left to a builder.

Once you've fixed the boundaries, try out a few quickly sketched plans to determine the basic shape of the kitchen (see below). At this stage, things should already be starting to fit into place.

THE CLASSIC LAYOUTS

The basic layout of the kitchen is usually dictated by the size and shape of the room.
U-shaped is the ideal. Using three sides of the room creates plenty of space while keeping everything conveniently close to hand.
Also, two people can work simultaneously without constantly crossing each other's paths.
L-shaped is the solution for a smaller room, where there isn't space for units on three sides, or for a large kitchen with separate working and eating/washing areas.
Galley/in-line layouts are the only choice for a room which is narrow or has a door at both ends.
Peninsulas or island units can help to keep the working area compact in a very large room.

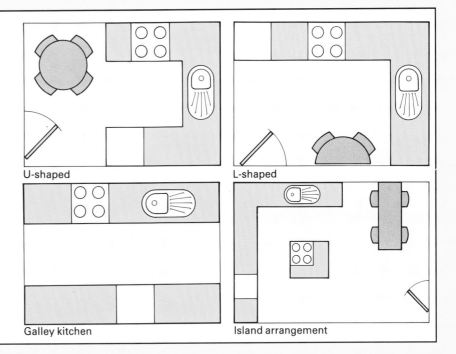

U-shaped

L-shaped

Galley kitchen

Island arrangement

ASSESSING NEEDS

Though you may not have much choice over the layout, there's plenty of scope for tailoring the kitchen to reflect your lifestyle. Some things probably spring immediately to mind. But to be sure nothing gets forgotten, it's worth listing your needs under the headings on the right.

Don't neglect future needs. There's no need to buy everything at once if your budget is tight, but extra units and appliances may be difficult to add later unless you plan for them at the outset.

What/how do you cook?
Think about how – and how often – you prepare:
■ Breakfast
■ Snacks and drinks
■ Simple family meals
■ Elaborate main meals
■ Food for freezing
Often the operations are very difficult; going through them can help you decide where your priorities lie.
Where space is tight, think about what could conveniently be left out of the kitchen – a freezer for example.

What other activities take place in the kitchen?
■ Will you be having snacks and meals there?
■ Do you need a separate area for washing and drying clothes?
■ Does the kitchen form the main thoroughfare to and from the garden?
■ Do you need space for young children to play?
Depending on the space available, it may help to think in terms of different activity zones and plan the layout accordingly to avoid collisions.

What might we want to add in the future?
■ Dishwasher
■ Freezer
■ Breakfast bar
■ Microwave
■ Separate oven/hob
■ Extra floor/wall units
As long as you apportion the space (and provide services where necessary), there's no reason why you can't fit a run of worktops and leave the space underneath empty. But don't plan things around existing appliances with only a limited life.

DRAWING A PLAN – THE CORE LAYOUT

Unless you've been given kitchen planning materials by the supplier, start by drawing a scale plan on 5mm squared paper (available as cheap scribble pads). Use a scale of 1:20 so that each square on the plan represents 100mm in real life.

Draw the outline of the room and the positions of fixtures being retained – doors, windows, boiler etc – in ink. Don't forget to mark on door opening swings.

From now on, you can either work in pencil and rub out, try out different layouts on tracing paper, or cut out the shapes of different units from a separate piece of squared paper and move them around on the plan. Most people find a pencil and rubber easiest.

Read the accompanying panels before going any further.

Where to start

It's usually easiest to start with the sink.
■ Its position is to a large extent governed by the existing drainage.

■ It is the focus of the work triangle.
■ Many people prefer it to be in front, or to one side, of a window.

With the sink in place (its exact position may be adjusted to fit units on either side) draw a line around the room representing the standard worktop depth – 600mm – and sketch in the units and appliances. Stick to what's available for your chosen range, or you may find yourself left with a 'missing link'.

Wall plans

Plans for each wall (elevations) can be drawn in the same way, using the same scale. You'll find it helpful to start by marking the worktop height – 900mm – and the wall unit height 400-500mm above it.

Sketch out plans on squared paper, adjusting positions of units and planning for alternative appliances, until you are happy with the layout. Then sketch an elevation (far right).

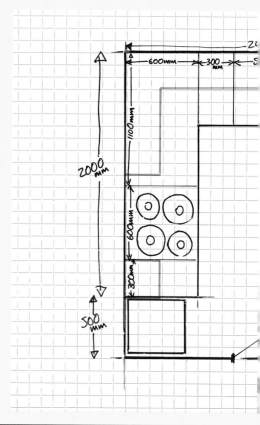

STANDARD DIMENSIONS

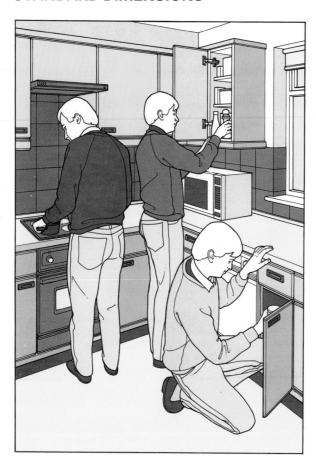

Standard proportions for kitchen units have been developed to suit the average person. Notice the kick space – without it you would have to twist your feet sideways to stand at the work surface.

Kitchen planning becomes much simpler if you remember that the vast majority of kitchen units are simple boxes, manufactured in a range of standard metric sizes. Appliances are sized accordingly (allowing clearance at the back, the sides, and for sliding under worktops), so groups of items should slot together neatly even though they don't fit the room exactly. The worktop is added to the units once they are fixed.

Floor-standing units are just under 600mm deep (to fit under standard 600mm deep worktops), and 900mm high (slightly adjustable in some cases). Widths are normally 300mm, 500mm, 600mm and 1000mm (increased to 1200mm in some ranges).

Standard carcases have an inset plinth providing all-important kick space, plus cut-outs at the back for running services.

Full-height units are the same depth, usually 1900mm to 2400mm high and 300mm, 500mm, or 600mm wide. *Oven and fridge housings* are 600mm wide.

Wall-hung units are normally half as deep as floor units – around 300mm – and come in the same widths. There are three heights – 300mm (called 'bridging' units), 600-700mm, and 900-1000mm. The units are designed to go 400-500mm above the work surface.

Sinks are normally fitted over a 1000mm double floor unit. With a flush fitting drainer you can use a narrower unit, but make sure there's space inside for the bowl and trap.

Built-under appliances normally fit a 'unit space' measuring 600mm wide by 600mm deep by 900mm high.

Slot-in cookers normally fit a 'unit space' 600mm wide by 600mm deep by 900mm high. '500mm' models are available for smaller kitchens.

Free-standing cookers are normally about 520mm wide – needing 20mm clearance on each side.

Free-standing fridges are usually 520mm wide.

Minimum distance between rows of units, an island or breakfast bar is 1200mm. Between rows of units and a wall, this can be reduced to around 900mm.

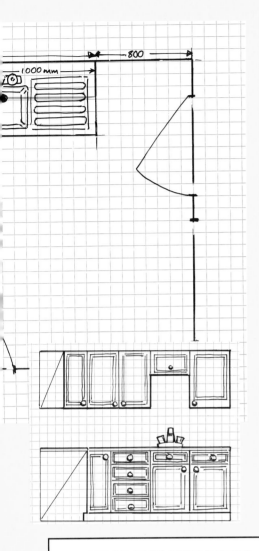

THE WORK TRIANGLE

When the cook is working in the kitchen, much of the time is spent walking between the three major work/storage areas – the cooker, the sink and the fridge. These three items form the corners of an imaginary 'work triangle' with worktop space in between. If they are fairly close together – even in a large kitchen – you not only save time and energy, but reduce the risk of accidents.

Taking your basic kitchen shape and the position of the sink as starting points, use the principle of the work triangle to plan the core of the layout. Though in practice the triangle may end up a straight line, the principle of easy movement between sink, cooker and fridge still applies.

Planning points
■ A trip around the triangle should be between 4 and 7 paces.
■ Site full-height appliances or units at the 'points' of the triangle – not in the middle.
■ Locate storage for often-used dry foods, crockery and kitchen utensils within the triangle.
■ Allow at least 600mm worktop space next to the sink and at least 400mm between a hob and full-height or oven unit.

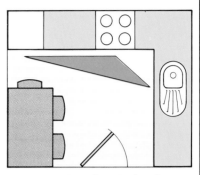

A classic L-shaped work triangle

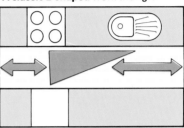

A throughway crossing the triangle

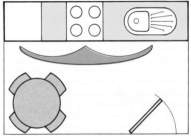

An in-line version of the triangle

WHAT ABOUT SERVICES?

It's vital to work out plumbing, gas and electricity requirements before the kitchen is installed, so that supplies can be rerouted where necessary.

Drainage If you plan to move the sink, the position of the drains may well be the deciding factor.
■ Mark the positions of gullies and drainage stacks on the plan.
■ Mark the route of the sink waste pipe to one or other outlet. As a rough guide it should be under 3m (9'9") long and have as few changes in direction as possible. It should also be hidden – usually by running behind a line of units.
Then, if required:
■ Mark the dishwasher position. This should be near the sink and can share the same waste pipe.
■ Mark the washing machine position. If there's room for a separate washing area, the machine could have its own waste pipe following a separate route to the stack or gully. Otherwise, position it near the sink to simplify the drainage. (A tumble drier normally needs a 100mm (4") vent direct to an outside wall, but condensing

models discharge via the washing machine waste.)

Water supplies are more flexible than drainage, but it's worth marking in prospective pipe runs to any appliances that need them. Take account of the present pipe positions, and try to keep new runs short and direct. Hide them behind units where possible.

Central heating may be a problem if there is a floor-mounted boiler or radiator in the way.
■ If the boiler could do with replacing, you might consider converting to a compact, wall-mounted model that can be incorporated in a run of wall units. But bear in mind that the job may be prohibitively costly unless you stick to more or less the same position.
■ A radiator should be easy to move. Alternatively, consider doing without it and diverting the pipes to supply a plinth-mounted electric fan heater.

Laying on gas supplies is a professional job. Installing a new supply is likely to be both costly and

disruptive. Moving an existing gas point could also prove difficult.

Electricity supplies need careful consideration – and possibly professional advice. Mark the positions of existing sockets, fused connection units (FCUs) and cooker control points. Then consider the following points:
■ Each fixed appliance needs a socket or FCU.
■ Each run of worktops needs at least one double socket (more, if you use a lot of kitchen gadgets).
■ Under-unit lights need their own supply; usually an FCU on the power circuit is most convenient.
■ An electric cooker or oven and hob need a control switch or box fed on a special circuit direct from the consumer unit.
Moving existing power points isn't difficult, so long as it is done before the kitchen units are fitted. Installing a lot of extra ones, however, may stretch the existing circuit wiring beyond its safe limit. The solution in such cases is to run a new radial or ring circuit from the consumer unit, exclusively for the kitchen. Take professional advice.

DRAWING A PLAN – FILLING IN THE SPACE

With the core layout established, work out how to fit in everything else. In small kitchens you will not have much choice when positioning appliances. Make sure all remaining spaces are accessible. In larger kitchens, the emphasis should be on keeping peripheral activities – clothes washing, eating, hobbies, through access – clear of the work triangle without sacrificing too much in the way of convenience.

Kitchen safety

Planning with safety in mind is particularly important if there are children or elderly people in the home, or if your kitchen has two doors and serves as a throughway.

■ Minimize the risk of fire in the kitchen by leaving the wall clear above a hob. Any cupboards you do put over the hob should be at least 800mm above it. Don't position the cooker or hob near a curtained window.

■ Keep the work triangle away from the main throughway to minimize the risk of collisions.

SEPARATING ACTIVITIES

Depending on the size of the kitchen, separation of the work triangle from other activity areas can be purely notional, or you can fit full-height units, a breakfast bar or island unit as physical dividers. What's important is that people doing different things in the kitchen don't keep crossing each other's paths, and that each activity has its own clearly defined worktop space, storage, and access route. For example, store tea, coffee and sugar near the fridge and kettle.

For a clothes washing area, try to arrange for the sink to be shared with the work triangle; this is more practical, and usually makes it easier to arrange services.

Children's play areas are often best divided off by a breakfast bar or peninsula to keep the work triangle physically separate.

Access to the garden means having a clear through route with somewhere to leave muddy shoes and put down odds and ends.

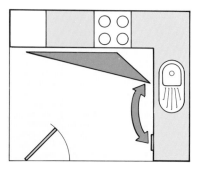

A clothes washing area should ideally share the sink with work triangle

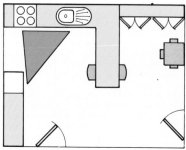

A breakfast bar provides a play area physically separate from the work triangle

SPACE SAVERS

If space is really tight, ask yourself again whether some appliances, storage, or activities can't be displaced to elsewhere in the house. Utility rooms, garages and outhouses make alternative sites for a washing machine, tumble drier or freezer and the area under the stairs might be capable of housing a freezer or some overspill storage. 'Best' china or glass may have a place in the living room. And does a built-in oven in a housing unit take up valuable work surface space?

There are also some classic space savers for the kitchen itself:

Carousels fitted into corner units give better access to storage space that might otherwise go to waste. You could use one to solve the problem of dry food storage within the work triangle.

A flap-down table on collapsible brackets provides space for quick breakfasts and snacks without blocking the main working layout.

A breakfast bar does more or less the same job, but may be a better choice where you have plenty of storage but lack worktop space.

Wall-mounted drainers can free worktop space around the washing-up area.

Open shelves and wall racks fit into non-standard spaces, to store appliances or decorative utensils.

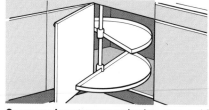
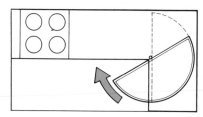

Space-saving storage: spinning carousel for a corner unit

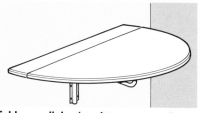
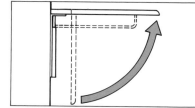

Foldaway dining/worktop space: a flap-down table

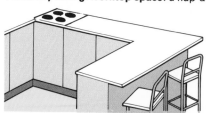
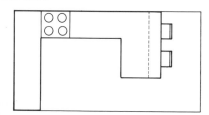

Dual purpose worktop: a breakfast bar and stools

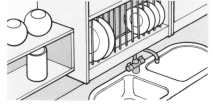
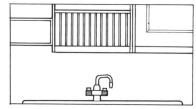

Wall-mounted storage: drainer rack and open shelves

FITTED KITCHENS – FITTING OUT THE CUPBOARDS

Basic kitchen units often provide no more than open shelves and drawers. And because these aren't always the best way to store all the things you use, kitchen designers have devised a range of fittings for all kinds of storage problems.

If you are planning a new kitchen, it's important to think about the uses you are going to put it to. Now's the time to decide whether fitting out the cupboards in a particular way will make the kitchen more convenient or give you more space.

The fittings shown below may be available as options for the range of units you buy. But if they aren't, or if you already have an existing fitted kitchen, you can still equip your cupboards with a range of kit equipment bought separately and added at any time.

Versions of all the fittings illustrated can be bought from specialist suppliers and fitted to standard sized kitchen unit carcases.

CHECKLIST: YOUR OPTIONS

SPECIAL PURPOSE FITTINGS

Fittings which save space or offer ingenious solutions to a number of familiar kitchen storage problems.

Extending table
Makes extra work-top space or a fold-away breakfast bar.

Mixer platform
Swings a mixer out from beneath base unit, ready for use.

Auto waste bin
Handy to use, and keeps rubbish out of sight.

Ironing board
Extendable and built in to save on storage space.

Scoop/drawer unit
Ideal for storing bulk ingredients in everyday use.

HANDY GADGETS

A range of small, inexpensive fittings to add to the convenience of your kitchen.

Spice rack
Makes use of unused space at the back of a worktop.

Cutlery insert
Can be used to organize odds and ends too.

Door opener
Gives automatic access to cupboards if hands are full.

Child-proof catches
For peace of mind when young children are about.

Towel rail
Fills an awkward corner and keeps towels close by.

SPACE FILLERS

Fittings designed to make better use of general storage areas – particularly hard-to-reach corners and unused spaces.

Carousel
Gives easy access to the inside of corner units.

Under-shelf storage
Open trays, baskets or boxes fit under wall units/shelves.

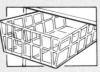
Pull-out unit
Puts things at the back of a cupboard within easy reach.

Plinth drawer
Makes use of the wasted space under base units.

Wire baskets
Organize small items in large, open cupboards.

MAKING THE MOST OF SPACE

Meeting kitchen storage needs can be a problem if you have to rely on the basic kitchen unit combination of drawers and open shelves. Small objects tend to get muddled or lost, and larger items often end up wasting valuable space.

The fittings shown here make the most of your existing storage by dividing it up more sensibly, or extending it into awkward corners that would otherwise go unfilled.

Trade tip

Storing buckets

❛ Many kitchen base units don't have enough room for a bucket or other large object because a shelf gets in the way. If you have this problem, fit a shallower shelf or use a jigsaw to take a scallop out of the shelf and then finish the cut with iron-on edging strip. ❜

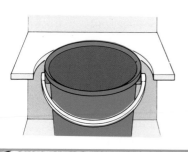

CAROUSELS/SWIVEL SHELVES

Carousels make it simple to store things in awkward corner cupboards. They consist of several swivelling shelves which may open with the door or pull out independently.

Different models have plastic trays or wire baskets. 'Half turn' semi-circular trays fit a straight corner unit. 'Three quarter' sets fit an L-shaped unit. You can also get mechanisms into which you fit your own shelves.

Planning points: Swivel shelves should fit a standard unit. Most types pivot on a pole fixed from top to bottom inside the cupboard, but some mechanisms are mounted on a hinged fixing plate.

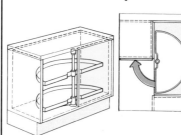

Half turn carousels have limited access as part of the shelf remains inside the cupboard.

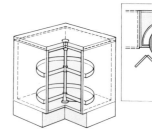

Three quarter turn carousels revolve fully for easy access to all parts of the shelves.

UNDER-SHELF STORAGE

Various items are available for fitting below a shelf to gain extra storage, or under a wall unit to free worktop space. The most common are wire trays, plastic boxes (bread bins) and plastic trays. Plastic trays may fit singly or come with wall mountings for fitting in stacks between a worktop and wall unit.

Planning points: If fitting to a wall unit, make sure you don't obstruct the cupboard doors above. Plan the storage to suit the working area below (ie bread bin over cutting board).

Wire baskets clip to any shelf.

WIRE BASKET SYSTEMS

Wire basket storage systems fit inside a conventional cupboard or pull-out unit. Various types are available in sizes to fit standard units. The two main alternatives are **drawer-type baskets** with runners that fit to the side panels of base units, and **free standing frames** with clip-on baskets.

Other useful fittings include wire baskets to fit on the back of doors or to side panels, and wire frames to fit around pull-out shelves. Use as open drawers for pan storage under hobs.
Planning points: Check the dimensions of your unit and what you need to store before choosing the baskets.

Wire drawers organize the space inside a plain carcase.

The runners are metal channels, screwed to the side panels.

PULL-OUT UNITS

Mechanisms for pull-out units are sold as accessories by some kitchen manufacturers. Existing plain pull-out drawers can also be fitted out with wire basket systems to make better use of the available space.

Larder units comprise a sturdy frame and runners designed to go inside a standard tall housing unit, plus wire baskets, plastic trays or shelves to aid storage.
Planning points: A pull-out needs space to extend, and you may need to reach both sides. Larder units are heavy and need extra wall fixings.

PLINTH DRAWERS

These fit under base units behind the plinth and are handy for storing things like cleaning materials. If plinth drawers aren't an option for your units, you may be able to fit your own based on a standard drawer kit.

Space under the units can also be used for storing folding steps – special models fold small enough to slip into a 90mm (3½″) space and there are easy-release brackets for the plinth panel if you store them here.
Planning point: Plinth drawers can only be fitted when you install the units. If you make your own from a drawer kit, fit false sides under the unit to take the drawer runners. Use edge-fitting drawer pulls to keep the original plinth look.

Plinth drawers have runners suspended under the unit's base.

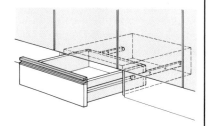

Make your own by fitting false sides as support for the runners.

SPECIAL PURPOSE FITTINGS

When storage or working space is limited, you may be able to make the kitchen more convenient with fold-away fittings. These are versions of commonly used equipment, designed to pack neatly away and swing into instant action.

The fittings shown here take up little more than a single drawer or shelf area. And because they fold up, they often occupy far less than the space needed to store and use a separate piece of equipment.

If fittings like these are part of a new kitchen system, remember to allow for them when you plan – sketch in their extended positions to check there is enough room. If you are fitting them to an existing kitchen, they are normally bought as kits which come complete with mounting brackets to screw to the inside of the base units.

MIXER PLATFORMS

Heavy kitchen appliances are awkward to keep in cupboards, but things like mixers and food processors take up valuable worktop space if they are left out.

A mixer platform goes inside a base unit like an ordinary shelf, but is suspended on a spring-loaded steel mechanism. This allows the shelf to pull forward and pivot up level with the worktop where it locks to bring the mixer (or other appliance) into instant use. When you've finished, the mixer simply swings back down for storage.

Planning points: You need at least 450mm (18″) height and 350mm (14″) depth inside the cupboard, and the unit fits inside any width from 300mm (12″) upwards. Make sure a power point is within reach.

A mixer platform is strong enough to support a heavy appliance in front of the worktop.

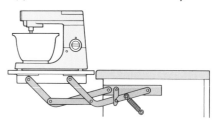

The mechanism pivots from the sides of the cupboard and folds down into the position of a shelf.

This type of bin screws to the door and has a string to open it.

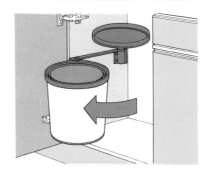

Other types of bin pull out of the cupboard, and are often much larger. They may prevent you from storing much else in the unit.

AUTOMATIC WASTE BINS

These fit inside base units and open with the cupboard door. And if you fit an automatic door opener too (see overleaf), the bin can be used even when your hands are full.

One type fits on the back of the cupboard door and has a string attachment to open the lid. Others go inside the unit and swing out behind the door.

Pull-out bins are often larger than other types and work like a large, deep drawer. You can also get open frames to take a plastic bin liner where space is critical.

Planning points: Size varies, but a typical bin may stand 400mm (16″) high and take up a space 300mm (12″) or so square.

A drawback with all automatic bins is that they prevent you from fitting a shelf in the unit or storing much else – for hygienic, as well as practical, reasons. And although they lift out for emptying, accidental spills inside the unit can be hard to clean.

SCOOP/DRAWER UNITS

These self-contained units are for storing basic ingredients like flour or sugar. Scoops have the advantage that they can dispense loose ingredients as you work. Similar sized drawer units are for small packs or things to spoon out.

Planning points: Site the unit over a worktop where it will be to hand when you need it. Avoid putting it where there's steam from a kettle or heat from a fridge vent.

This scoop unit fits on the wall above a worktop.

IRONING BOARDS

A pull-out ironing board normally replaces one of the drawers in a base unit, but where there are no drawers it can also be fitted under a worktop, behind one of the unit doors. The mechanism allows the board to fold up into the depth of a normal cupboard, but extends outwards and upwards to make a full-size ironing board.

The outer frame is fixed to the inside of the base unit in a similar way to ordinary drawer runners and the front of the frame is designed so that a standard drawer front simply screws on. No extra support is needed, and there are no legs to get in the way.

Planning points: Make sure you have enough room to work all round the extended board. A typical size is about 320mm (13″) wide, projecting out around 950mm (38″) from the worktop, and you need about 600mm (24″) clear space on either side. Make sure there is a power point within easy reach of the iron flex. You can fit the iron on a wall-mounted caddy nearby.

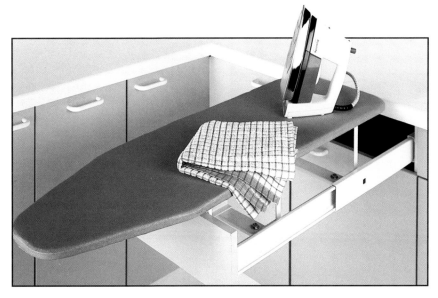

When closed, the ironing board fits a standard drawer space.

Extension runners allow it to pull out and up for instant use.

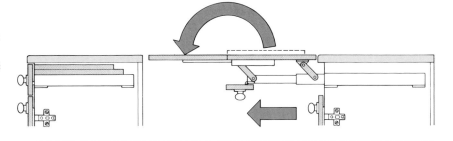

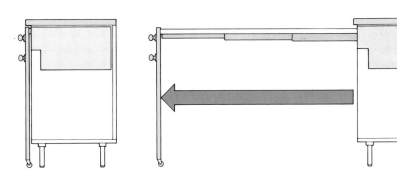

The runner mechanism (below) pulls out the table in sections so it extends from the worktop.

On long tables (above) you need front supporting legs or a false front which runs out on castors.

EXTENDING TABLES

Extending tables can be used to create an extra working area, or to make a breakfast bar that packs away under the worktop.

There are various designs and sizes, but all of them work in a similar way. The table is concealed inside a base unit so that when you pull out the 'drawer' front, the table top extends outwards. A folding mechanism inside allows the table top to be much longer than the 600mm (24″) or so depth of the unit, but the length when extended varies.

Short tables are often supplied as self-contained kits which simply screw to the inside of the cabinet in the space left by the drawer. The drawer front then attaches to the front of the unit.

Longer tables also need an end support. This can be a pair of separate extending legs, or you can attach both the drawer and door panels to the mechanism, creating a 'false front' for the base unit that pulls forward on castors to support the table as it extends.

Planning point: Make sure you have enough room – not just in front of the cupboard, but on either side too. You need around 700mm (28″) to pull a chair up to a table.

HANDY GADGETS

The kick-plate releases a catch which holds the base of the door.

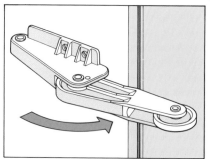

A spring-loaded opener pushes the door forward when released.

DOOR OPENERS

These allow doors or pull-out units to be opened 'hands-off' and are very useful for automatic waste bins. The door or pull-out is held back against a spring loaded opener, and is released by a kick-plate fitted in front of the base unit plinth which you operate with your toe.

Planning points: Very little space is occupied by the mechanism, which should fit any standard unit.

TOWEL RAILS

Pull-out towel rails fit under the worktop. They are screwed to the side of a cabinet, the underside of a worktop, or the back wall. The rail extends to bring the towels into easy reach and different numbers of arms are available.

Planning point: Little space is needed and a rail can be used in any small gap between units. But make sure you have enough hanging space below the rails.

CUTLERY INSERTS

These plastic mouldings with divisions for knives, forks and spoons are neater than a separate tray. There are several standard sizes as well as universal patterns which you trim to fit the drawer exactly, using a sharp knife and sandpaper, or a planer.

Planning point: Either buy one that fits exactly or the next largest insert. The depth is normally around 60mm (2½").

CHILD-PROOF CATCHES

Springy door catches stop small children opening cupboard doors but are easy for an adult to release. Similar drawer stops can be fitted under the worktop to stop drawers from being pulled right out.

Planning point: Door catches allow some leeway for adjustment but they can be tricky to align. If you are installing new units, make sure you align the doors properly **before** fitting catches.

Press the plastic catch to open the door beyond a small amount.

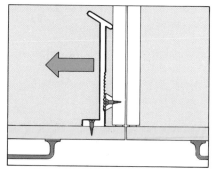

The two parts must be adjusted so that they align accurately.

SPICE RACKS

These are for fitting to the backs of cupboard doors or to the space between worktop and wall units.

Planning point: Try a sample of your spice jars to ensure they fit snugly and won't fall out. Keep wall-mounted units out of the sun.

INDEX

A
Abrasive paper, 32
Accessories:
 kitchen cupboards, 73-8
 wardrobes, 47-52
Alcoves:
 built-in furniture, 39
 glass shelving, 29, 30
 shelves, 7, 8, 19-24
 wardrobes, 54
Aluminium angle supports, 21, 23
Aluminium brackets, 11
Aluminium channel shelves, 15, 16, 30

B
Basins, 36, 38
Bathroom storage, 8, 31, 36
Baths, boxed-in, 36
Battens:
 alcove shelving, 21, 22
 bracket shelving, 14
 built-in furniture, 38
 glass shelving, 29, 32
 track shelving, 26, 28
Bedhead units, 59
Bedrooms:
 built-in wardrobes, 41
 cupboards, 33, 35
 modular furniture, 59-64
 shelving, 9
 sliding wardrobe doors, 53-8
 wardrobe accessories, 47-52
Bifold doors, 36
Blockboard:
 built-in furniture, 38
 lining alcoves, 24
 shelves, 13, 20
Bookcase strip, 21, 23
Bookends, track shelving, 25
Box units, 37
 track shelving, 28
Bracketless shelving, 15-18, 30
Brackets, 7, 11, 12, 13, 29, 30
 alcove shelving, 21, 23
 bracket shelves, 11-14
 cantilever, 15, 17
 glass shelving, 29, 30, 32
 radiator shelves, 18
 track shelving, 25
Breakfast bars, 72, 77
Bridging units, modular furniture, 59, 61
Built-in furniture:
 cupboards, 33, 37-42
 kitchen units, 65-8
 wardrobes, 35, 41
Bunk beds, 35

C
Cantilever brackets, 15, 17
Carousels, 72, 73, 74
Chests of drawers, 38, 61
Children's rooms, 8, 9, 35
Chimney breasts, 20
Chipboard:
 built-in furniture, 38
 drawer fronts, 43

 lining alcoves, 24
 shelves, 13, 20
Clothes, wardrobe storage, 47-52
Concertina doors, 36
Corner units:
 carousels, 72, 73, 74
 modular furniture, 59, 61
Cornices, 39, 64
Cube storage, 33
Cupboards, 33-6
 built-in, 37-42
 doors, 36
 fitted kitchen units, 65-8
 fitting out kitchen cupboards, 73-8
 fitting out wardrobes, 47-52
 modular bedroom furniture, 59-64
 sliding doors, 53-8
 types, 33
Cutlery inserts, 73, 78
Cutting shelves, 24

D
Dishwashers, 71
Dividing rooms, 10, 31
Doors:
 airing cupboards, 42
 automatic openers, 73, 76, 78
 built-in furniture, 38, 39
 built-in wardrobes, 41
 child-proof catches, 73, 78
 kitchen units, 40
 modular bedroom furniture, 60, 63
 sliding, 53-8
Downlighters, 30
Drawers:
 built-in furniture, 38
 child-proof catches, 78
 cutlery inserts, 73, 78
 dressing tables, 41
 kit drawers, 43-6
 modular units, 59, 61, 63
 plinth, 73, 75
 scoop/drawer units, 73, 76
 wardrobes, 47, 48, 51
Dressing tables, 38, 41, 59, 60, 62

F
Faced chipboard, 38
Fitted cupboards, 33
Fixings, brackets, 11
Floating shelves, 7
Fluorescent lighting, 36
Framed furniture, built-in, 37
Free-standing cupboards, 33
Free-standing shelves, 7

G
Garages, 10
Glass fixing pads, 13, 32
Glass-fronted cupboards, 34
Glass shelves, 13, 29-32
 across windows, 8, 29, 31
 aluminium channels, 16
Glides, drawers, 44

H
Halls, cupboards, 36

Halogen lighting, 30
Handles, modular bedroom furniture, 64
Hanging plates, 15, 18
Hanging rails:
 extending, 52
 modular bedroom furniture, 63
 wardrobes, 47-50
Hardboard, built-in furniture, 38
Headboards, 59
Hi-fi equipment, 8, 19
Hinges:
 kitchen units, 40
 modular bedroom furniture, 63
Hot water cylinders, 42

I
Infill strips, track shelving, 25
Ironing boards, 73, 77

K
Kitchens:
 built-in units, 40
 cupboards, 34
 fitted units, 65-8
 fitting out cupboards, 73-8
 layouts, 69-72
 shelves, 8, 9

L
Laminated softwood boards, 12, 15, 20
Landings, 10, 36
Larder units, 75
Lighting:
 deep cupboards, 36
 illuminated shelving, 30
 kitchen planning, 71
Lining alcoves, 24
Lipping, 13, 28
Living rooms:
 built-in furniture, 39
 cupboards, 34
 shelves, 8
Louvre doors, airing cupboards, 42

M
Man-made boards, 13
MDF (medium density fibreboard):
 built-in furniture, 38
 lining alcoves, 24
 shelves, 13, 20
Medicine cupboards, 36
Melamine faced boards, 13, 15
Metal channels:
 aluminium channel shelves, 15, 16, 30
 glass shelving, 29
Mirrors, sliding wardrobe doors, 54
Mixer platforms, 73, 76
Modular units:
 bedroom furniture, 59-64
 cupboards, 33, 34, 37
Mouldings:
 built-in furniture, 38, 39
 drawer fronts, 43
 modular bedroom furniture, 6

O

Oilstones, 32

P

Panels, drawer fronts, 43
Picture rails, 39
Planning:
  built-in furniture, 38
  kitchens, 65, 68, 69-72
  modular bedroom furniture, 60
Plasterboard, built-in furniture, 38
Plastic coated chipboard, 20
Plinths:
  drawers, 73, 75
  kitchen units, 40
  living room units, 39
  modular bedroom furniture, 64
Plug-in end supports, 29
Plug-in shelf supports, 21
Plywood:
  built-in furniture, 38
  lining alcoves, 24
  shelves, 13, 20
Pull-out units, kitchens, 73, 75

R

Radiators:
  kitchen planning, 71
  shelves above, 8, 18
Rails:
  extending, 52
  modular bedroom furniture, 63
  towel rails, 73, 78
  wardrobes, 47-50
Ramin lipping, 28
Rollers, drawers, 45
Runners:
  drawers, 44, 45
  plinth drawers, 75
  wire baskets, 75

S

Scale plans:
  built-in furniture, 38

kitchens, 69-72
modular bedroom furniture, 60
Scoop/drawer units, 73, 76
Scotia moulding, 64
Shelves:
  alcoves, 7, 8, 19-24
  bracket, 11-14
  bracketless, 15-18, 30
  enclosed, 7
  floating, 7
  free-standing, 7
  glass, 29-32
  in kitchens, 8, 9
  modular furniture, 59, 63
  radiator, 8, 18
  strengthening, 28
  track, 7, 25-8
  under-shelf storage, 73, 74
  unenclosed, 7
  wardrobes, 47, 48, 50, 51
Skirting boards, 39, 58
Sliding doors, 53-8
Softwood:
  built-in furniture, 38
  drawer fronts, 43
  shelves, 12, 15
Softwood lipping, 28
Spice racks, 73, 78
Stairs, storage under, 10, 36
'Streamlined' brackets, 11
Strengthening shelves, 28
Strip lighting, 30, 36
Stud walls, 26, 27

T

Tables:
  extending, 73, 77
  flap-down, 72
  height, 38
Televisions, 8, 19
Towel rails, 73, 78
Tracks:
  alcove shelving, 21, 23
  glass shelving, 29, 32

shelving systems, 7, 25-8
sliding doors, 55-6
Trims, modular bedroom furniture, 64
Tumble driers, 71, 72
Tungsten strip lighting, 36

U

Unenclosed shelves, 7

V

Veneered boards, 13, 20, 38, 43
Vertical panels, track shelving, 28

W

Wallplugs, 15
Walls, uneven, 13, 24, 26, 28
Wardrobes:
  built-in, 35, 41
  fitting out, 47-52
  modular units, 61, 62
  sliding doors, 53-8
Washbasins, height, 38
Washing machines, 34, 71, 72
Waste bins, automatic, 73, 76, 78
Water, kitchen planning, 71
Wet or dry abrasive paper, 32
Windows:
  cupboards around, 35
  glass shelves, 8, 29, 31
Wire baskets:
  kitchens, 73, 75
  wardrobes, 47, 48, 49, 52
Wood:
  brackets, 11, 12
  drawer fronts, 43
  lipping, 28
  shelves, 12, 20
Worktops:
  built-in furniture, 38
  dressing tables, 41
  kitchen planning, 40, 71, 72
  modular furniture, 59, 63

ACKNOWLEDGEMENTS

Photographers
Acmetrack Ltd 47-48, 49(t) 53-55, 57; B & Q 12(b); Richard Burbidge 23(b); Domestic Storage Systems 33(bl); Dulux 1(br), 8, 67(b); Eaglemoss 25(b), (Jon Bouchier) 23(c), (Derek St Romaine) 43-44, (John Suett) front cover(bl) 15-17, 20, 23(t), 24, 32, (Steve Tanner) 11(b), 78(tl), 78(b); Gower Fern 61, 65; Robert Harding Picture Library 2; Homecharm 73, 76, 77(b), 78(c); Kingswood 67(t); The Kitchen Consultancy front cover(tr); Lancelot 35(t); Magnet 60, 76(b); MFI 10(b), 35(b), 59, 66(b), 68; National Magazine Company/Good Housekeeping 11(t), 19; Sharp 33(br);

Smallbone 1(tl); Spur Shelving Ltd 12-13(t), 13(b), 25(t), 26-27; Stag 34; Texas Homecare front cover(br), 66(t); Elizabeth Whiting Associates 6, 9, 22, 29-31, 37, (Michael Dunne) 4; Wickes 10(t), 36, 49(b), 74, 75(t); Woodfit 78(tr); Wrighton 75(b), 77(t).

Illustrators
Kuo Kang Chen 19-24; Paul Cooper 53-58; Jeremy Dawkins 73-78; Paul Emra 7-10, 25-28, 29-32, 33-36, 47-52; Mick Gillah 73-78; Andrew Green 11-14, 15-18, 53-58, 73-78; Maltings Partnership front cover(tl); Stan North 37-42, 43-46, 59-64, 69-72; Colin Salmon 53-58; Peter Serjeant 11-14.